the assassin
from apricot city

the assassin from apricot city

reportage from Turkey

by Witold Szabłowski

translated by Antonia Lloyd-Jones

STORK PRESS

Published by
Stork Press Ltd
170 Lymington Avenue
London
N22 6JG

www.storkpress.co.uk

English edition first published 2013 by Stork Press
1

Translated from the original *Zabójca z miasta moreli* © Witold Szabłowski, 2010
English translation © Antonia Lloyd-Jones, 2013

ENGLISH PEN | Supported using public funding by **ARTS COUNCIL ENGLAND**

This book has been selected to receive financial assistance from English PEN's "PEN Translates!" programme, supported by Arts Council England. English PEN exists to promote literature and our understanding of it, to uphold writers' freedoms around the world, to campaign against the persecution and imprisonment of writers for stating their views, and to promote the friendly co-operation of writers and the free exchange of ideas. www.englishpen.org

Polish Cultural Institute London

The publisher gratefully acknowledges assistance from the Polish Cultural Institute in London for its support towards the publication of this book.

The moral right of the author has been asserted

These characters are fictional and any resemblance to any persons living or dead is entirely coincidental

All rights reserved

No part of this publication may be reproduced, stored in or introduced into a retrieval system, or transmitted, in any form or by any means (electronic, mechanical, photocopying, recording or otherwise), without the prior written permission of both the copyright owner and the publisher of this book

Paperback ISBN 978-0-9573912-5-3
ebook ISBN 978-0-9573912-5-3

Designed and typeset by Mark Stevens in 10.5 on 13 pt Athelas Regular

Printed in the UK by MPG Books Group Ltd

acknowledgements

Aylin Aras, Jadwiga Dąbrowska, the editors of Duży Format, *Serhat Guneş, Agnieszka Koecher-Hensel, Izabela Meyza, Zubeyde Öztürk, Beata Uzunkaya, and Magdalena Wojcieszak-Çopuroğlu.*

Sevgili arkadaşlar, sizler olmasaydınız bu kitap olamazdı. Çok teşekkür ederim.

contents

Map	viii
Pronunciation	xi
Instead of a preface	xv
Taksim tales	1
The purgatory of Istanbul	15
It's out of love, sister	35
Sinan's dream	59
Imams and condoms	65
At the foot of Mount Ararat	81
Moustachioed republic	87
Madame Atatürk	107
The black girl	113
Abraham's carp	133
The assassin from apricot city	141
Bye Bye Bush	161
Nazım	179
That's Turkey for you	209

BULGARIA
GREECE
Edirne
Kırklareli
Tekirdağ
Istanbul
İzmit
Adapazari
Düzce
Bolu
Zonguldak
Bartın
Karabük
Kastamonu
Sinop
Çankırı
Çorum
Çanakkale
Bursa
Bilecik
Ankara
Eskişehir
Kırıkkale
Yozga
Ayvalık
Balıkesir
Kütahya
Kırşehir
Manisa
Afyon
Nevşehir
Usak
Izmir
Aydın
Denizli
Isparta
Burdur
Konya
Niğde
Muğla
Karaman
Antalya
Adan
Mersin
Cyprus
Mediterranean Sea

RUSSIA
GEORGIA
AZERBAIJAN
ARMENIA
IRAN
IRAQ
SYRIA
ANON
TURKEY
Black Sea
sun
Ordu
Giresun
Trabzon
Rize
Artvin
Ardahan
Kars
asya
Tokat
Gümüşhane
Bayburt
Erzurum
Iğdır
Sivas
Erzincan
Ağrı
Tuneceli
Bingöl
Mus
Elazığ
Malatya
Van
Bitlis
Diyarbakır
Siirt
Batman
hramanmaraş
Adıyaman
Simak
Hakkâri
Mardin
Şanlıurfa
Gaziantep
Kilis
takya

pronunciation

THE TURKISH c sounds like the English j. Thus the name of the Ottoman general Mustafa Celaleddin should be read as 'Jelaleddin'. The man's name Cemal is read as 'Jemal' and the woman's name Hatice as 'Hatije'.

The letter ğ lengthens the vowel preceding it. Thus the surname of Ali Ağca, the assassin who shot Pope John Paul II, is pronounced 'Aaja'.

Ş and ç are like English sh and ch. Thus the names of the cities Şile and Çanakkale sound like 'Shi-le' and 'Chanakka-le'.

The letter ı is like an English y, so the name Nazım sounds like 'Nazym'.

Ö and ü sound the same as in German, pronounced with slightly pursed lips.

Coffee was drunk by many of the Polish envoys and soldiers who came into contact with the Turks. However, it was generally regarded as a pagan invention, not to say satanic. It was black, bitter, and bad. Only when it came to us from Paris and Amsterdam did drinking it start to be regarded as the height of elegance.
    Jarosław Dumanowski, expert on the history of food and cuisine, in a Polish newspaper interview

Asteroid B-612 has only once been seen through the telescope. That was by a Turkish astronomer, in 1909. On making his discovery, the astronomer had presented it to the International Astronomical Congress, in a great demonstration. But he was in Turkish costume, and so nobody would believe what he said. ... Fortunately, however, a Turkish dictator made a law that his subjects, under pain of death, should change to European costume. So in 1920 the astronomer gave his demonstration all over again, dressed with impressive style and elegance. And this time everybody accepted his report.
    Antoine de Saint-Exupéry, *The Little Prince*, Chapter 4, translated by Katherine Woods.

I feel as if I'm always on a bridge connecting the two sides of the Bosporus without belonging either to the Asian or the European side, and writing about both of them.
    Orhan Pamuk

instead of a preface

THE YELLOW AND WHITE FERRY wheezes, groans, spits a cloud of smoke into the sky and moves off.

We are sailing from Europe to Asia. The journey takes about a quarter of an hour. Here there are businessmen along with beggars, women in chadors with women in mini-skirts, non-believers with Imams, prostitutes with dervishes, the holy with the unholy – all Turkey on a single ferry.

'The captains of these giants are the modern-day Charons,' says Tayfun, a poet friend of mine from Istanbul. 'Why? Because the journey across the Bosporus is both beautiful and alarming. Like death.'

In fact the Charons are cool professionals. Otherwise their job would be impossible. The Bosporus is very narrow, in some places barely a few hundred metres wide, but there are thousands of boats and ships going past each other here. Manoeuvring on these waters, and finally steering a huge ferry straight, to the last centimetre, into a small berth – here there is no room for Romanticism or Greek mythology.

Well, unless you are a passenger. In which case, be my guest. When dusk falls and thousands of muezzins start to proclaim that Allah is great, the conversations cease and people sink into a melancholy, metaphysical mood. I often take advantage of this to ask a few random Turks: 'What's it like living with this strait? Is anybody here interested in the daily journey between continents?'

They shrug their shoulders. They don't understand what I'm asking. A strait is a strait.

Only Tayfun the poet isn't in the least surprised by the question.

'I have a sort of strait inside me too,' he says, throwing a large piece of pretzel towards the seagulls chasing the ferry. 'Every Turk hovers between tradition and modernity a thousand times a day – the hat or the *charshaf* [veil]; the mosque or the disco; the European Union or dislike of the European Union.'

He has hit the nail on the head. The whole of Turkey is torn in half by an invisible strait. In the morning my female friends drink espressos with their boyfriends, eat croissants and talk about world literature. Then in the afternoon they put on their headscarves and go to their grandmothers' houses for Turkish coffee.

My male friends will grab a beer and have fun at the disco. But as they drink, they sing songs from two hundred years ago. They act like tough guys who aren't afraid of Allah or Mohammed, but at Ramadan they dutifully fast, and when their sons grow up a bit, they rush off to have them circumcised.

In the conservative east of the country I myself have seen imams who fly the European Union flag outside their mosques, and shops with clothes for conservative Turkish women will have sexy underwear on sale. 'If a woman covers her face the entire day,' the salesmen explain, 'they're all the more keen to please their husbands at night.'

Being on the border has its advantages. The Turks are creative and quick to learn languages, instantly able to win over people from a wide geographical latitude. Although they are in the worst position imaginable – sharing a border with restless Syria, Iran and Iraq, they are simultaneously part of the Middle East, the Caucasus and the Balkans – they are able to get on well with almost everyone.

But this life on the border has its price. The West regards them as fanatics, and the East as lackeys of the West. Al-Qaida carries out terrorist attacks in Turkey, and for half a century the European Union has refused to accept the country as a member, because it is too big and too culturally alien.

Our ferry has reached the middle of the strait. In the distance we can see the two bridges which straddle the shores of the Bosporus. Tayfun the poet gazes first at the European side, then at the Asian. Finally he sighs and says: 'Every Turk is a bridge like that.'

taksim tales

'OUR PRIME MINISTER IS AN ISLAMIST, a thug, and a danger to the country. We must get rid of him at the first opportunity,' said the people occupying Gezi Park.

'Rubbish! He's a genius! He was sent to us from heaven!' said the people who didn't go to the park.

It's June, 2013. I've brought a sleeping bag, a camping mat and a thermos flask, and come to talk to both sides of the argument. What unites them, and what divides them? And how will the occupation of the park leave its mark on them in general?

two tribes

Gezi Park adjoins a four-lane road; at the centre of the park there's a fountain, and at each corner there are luxury hotels. The Istanbul city authorities – and the Turkish government too – want to dig it up and build a shopping mall on the site, designed to look like a military barracks from the Ottoman era. And so this is where, in late May 2013, Turkey's young people held their first protest, which was brutally suppressed by the police.

In response, thousands more young Turks were drawn to Gezi Park, where they pitched their tents and proceeded to occupy the place. Their demonstration in defence of the park soon evolved into a protest against the government which, to their minds, fails to listen to the citizens, is changing Turkey into an Islamic state and taking an increasingly authoritarian approach. Expelled by the police several times and branded by the Turkish prime minister as vandals, they keep coming back to the park.

To the despair of the owners of the five-star hotels, which for over a fortnight now have been suffering losses. When the protests began, their well-heeled guests could order gas masks at the reception desk – the effects of the tear gas sprayed by the police could be felt in the rooms.

The well-heeled guests were in Istanbul on business, or for a special shopping month, with major price reductions and round-the-clock opening hours. But instead of that, there were riots and tear gas, which irritated the eyes, nose, larynx and sinuses. Whenever they could feel it, the guests went onto their hotel verandas, from where they had a perfect view of:

- crowds of rebellious young Turks gathered inside the park, with long hair and moustaches – recently back in fashion – as well as guitars and placards with pictures of Prime Minister Recep Tayyip Erdoğan's face crossed out; and
- some slightly older Turks, with pot bellies, in suits of varying quality, each with a cigarette in one hand, and an Islamic string of beads for evoking the name of Allah in the other, intense and agitated, walking around the outside of the park.

'Turkey is divided right down the middle, into two tribes,' says sociology student Zübeyde Topbaş as she gazes at the people with pot bellies from the red tent in which she is occupying Gezi Park. We're sitting on sleeping mats inside her tent, while two tents further along someone's playing songs dating back to Atatürk's revolution on a stringed instrument called the bağlama.

Twenty-three-year-old Zübeyde, who has long black hair and a dark complexion, only joined the protest on the third day. 'Before then I didn't believe anything would come of it. My friends have been saying for years that they've had enough of our ruling party. I've heard the same comments every time the Justice and Development Party (the AKP) members of parliament have tried to introduce flogging as a punishment for adultery. It was the same when they banned teaching about evolution, and when they introduced headscarves to schools. I thought it would just end in hot air again. Because until now every debate has ended with the fact that they're the ones who've given us economic growth. They're the ones fighting for us to join the European Union. So what if they talk about Islam a lot in the process? Evidently in this country it's impossible to do otherwise.'

It was only when Zübeyde saw what was really going on in the park adjacent to Taksim Square, the focal point of the city, on the BBC news – because initially the Turkish media didn't say a word about the protests – that she packed her rucksack, found the pegs for the tent she hadn't used for ages, and went off with a friend to occupy Gezi Park. The very first day she posted a picture of them sitting in the tent on Facebook, with a short tag: #occupygezi. Never had any of her pictures received so many likes – 500 in the space of fifteen minutes. 'It was liked by a huge number of people I've never met – I didn't even know that was possible. That set me thinking,' says Zübeyde. 'My emotions went through the roof. The most dangerous thing right now is that instead of trying to close the divide between the Turks, our politicians are consciously widening it. I'm quite sure Erdoğan has cynically taken advantage of our protest to win the local council elections next year. To consolidate the people who vote for him, who still far outnumber those who think like us. Like

Putin, who won the Russian elections in the 1990s by striking out at the Chechens. We haven't any Chechens, lately there's been peace with the Kurds, but even so it's possible to set one lot of Turks against the other. Non-believers against believers. Liberals against socialists. Rich against poor.'

'Then why the protest, if in your view it serves the government?'

'What alternative do we have?' says Zübeyde, playing with a lock of hair. 'Agree to his ideas again? Pretend nothing has happened? Pretend you can build a mosque at the heart of a secular state and get away with it?'

'He talked about the mosque in the run-up to the last elections, and he won them.'

'We've already got a hundred times more mosques than hospitals or schools. Culture here is in dire straits, there's no money for the theatre. But they'll always find enough to build a mosque. If you want a successful career in local government, you have to go to Friday prayers. Best of all during working hours, so your bosses will see you there. So I'm sorry, but we can't possibly agree to yet another mosque.'

pretty boys

'The mosque doesn't bother me at all. They can put it next to Gezi Park if they like. The only thing I don't get is why Tayyip's so keen to do away with our park entirely,' says Tayfun in a reedy voice, almost falsetto, bending his hand at the wrist in such an exaggerated way that I can't tell if he's emphasising his own sexual orientation or on the contrary, sending up the gays in an offensive way. We are sitting at the outpost of an organisation that fights for homosexual rights. They have two small tables in the park, where you can talk to a transsexual, for example. They're handing out free condoms and... cheese sandwiches. 'Tayyip's got such a nice bum! And he's so sexy when he gets angry...' Tayfun fantasises, as if he's forgotten he's talking about Turkey's conservative prime minister, who would probably rather die than be complimented by a gay. 'I'll tell you a secret,' he says, leaning forwards to whisper in my ear. 'He's closing down Gezi Park because of me.'

'What do you mean, because of you?'

'Well, because of me and my friends. We come here to shag,' laughs Tayfun, and I have a moment to take a good look at him. I'd say he's just over forty, in tight jeans, a studded belt and a T-shirt with a rainbow flag on it, and his chest is shaved. 'Pretty boys from all over the city come here. And also a few queens and trannies. Gezi is famous for it all over Turkey, and Tayyip knows that – after all, he grew up a stone's throw from here,' says Tayfun, pointing towards the Kasımpaşa district, where the Turkish prime minister did indeed grow up.

The fact that Gezi Park fell into Erdoğan's disfavour because of gay excesses is something I have heard from my Turkish journalist friends before now. The gays have got to go, because a mosque is going to be built right next to this place. The best way to be rid of them is to close down the park, fence it off and build something in the middle.

'Ever since they threw us out of Gezi all the queens have been standing in the side streets. Tayyip is having them bring in excavators and bulldozers to build some wretched Ottoman barracks. But somehow I can't get angry with him, even though he's bloody well gassed us. That's me all over – always smiling. When I was still living in Konya – that's where I was born – they used to call me a queen. People there are ignorant, they can't tell the difference between a faggot and a queen, and I simply hadn't the strength to explain. I had to get out of there, or they'd have beaten me to death.

'So I came to Istanbul, and moved in with this old gay who couldn't walk any more. Every day I took him to Gezi in his wheelchair. He couldn't be active any more, but he wanted to get a look at least. He asked me to bury him here because, as he said, this was where he'd had the finest times of his life. But it didn't work out, and a good thing too, because now they'd be digging him up with those excavators. And gassing him too. The first time the police came, the queens from the park started calling Tayyip rude names, saying he's a dictator and a fascist for sending the police out against us. But I'm not like that, I don't go calling people fascist. So I told them: "Who sent you all these lovely policemen? Just look, because it might be the loveliest sight you ever see. Just look at them wiggling their bums as they whack you with their truncheons! Just look, and thank your lucky stars for Tayyip, who gave us all this!"'

grenade in a shopping bag

But most encounters with the police have been far less pleasant.

The day before their harshest attack on the people occupying Gezi Park, a man tried to foist a grenade on Mustafa, a law student from near Izmir. 'He said he was a soldier who had deserted his unit on the wave of protests, and had stolen a few pieces of ammunition. He shoved an object into my shopping bag; he said it was a grenade. He kept trying to persuade us we had to have grenades to defend ourselves because the police were going to liquidate us without mercy,' says Mustafa. 'What did we do? I didn't even want to touch the thing. And my friends wanted to give him a thrashing. We knew he was a nark or an agitator. What's more, he was tremendously dumb, because he was trying to make this offer at a peace camp – look at the great big A in a circle hanging right above the entrance. A weapon was the last thing he could possibly have pressed on us. Eventually he ran off, and we chased him halfway across the park, shouting: "Get lost!"

'I don't even want to think what would have happened if they'd found that grenade on us. The police were just waiting for something like that! People like that man have been coming here every day. A friend of mine kept seeing this one guy. Whenever there was conflict with the police, he was there, throwing firebombs at them. But later, when my friend was escorted to a police van, that same guy kicked him in the guts. He hadn't even changed his shirt.'

'But why should the police want to provoke you, Mustafa?'

'Because you can't apply force and tear gas to people of a peaceful nature. It looks bad – you should be talking to them. There's nobody here but peace freaks. We've been sitting here for a fortnight, and besides politics, we talk about veganism, and fruitarianism, and we watch films – five cinemas have opened in the park. We've got a debating club, a legal advice point, a masseuse and a hairdresser. There's nothing suspicious going on. Anyway, I promised my mum I wouldn't get dragged into anything stupid. My mum brought me up on her own, and I owe her a lot. Life is not at all easy for single mothers in Turkey, because it's part of our culture that a woman only matters when she's got a husband to back her up. So when my mum said: "Son, perhaps you'd better not go to the park", I replied: "I'm going there for you, Mum. If those yokels from the AKP go on running the country, it'll just get worse and worse for women like you. I'm sitting here for your sake, and I promise everything will be fine."

'And it is. Look how many people have set up business selling koftas and tea. If we had sharp teeth, they'd be afraid and they'd stay away. And it would only take one of those grenades to accuse us of all the worst crimes on earth and lock us up for five hundred years.'

democracy in tough times

'They're not in the least well-behaved. You should have seen them robbing my shop. I'd run that scum over with a steamroller,' rages Metin the shopkeeper. His shop of the type selling soap, jam, chewing gum and various kinds of alcohol is located right next to Taksim Square, but has been closed for over a week. First the people occupying Gezi Square took several packets of biscuits without paying, then they spray-painted the shop window, and finally they wrote some obscene words on the security shutters, so he has suffered considerable losses. On top of that he feels extremely resentful. He thinks nobody is listening to people like him, who vote for Erdoğan's party and who side with the prime minister. 'I've been watching the foreign news reports, showing the young Turks fighting against authoritarian power, and I can't believe what I'm hearing. Taksim Square is like Tahrir Square in Cairo? You people in the West should go and get your EU heads tested! Can a prime minister who has won three parliamentary elections and two referenda, and whose man is president of the country – can a prime minister like that be compared to Mubarak? I realise people have the right to defend the park. But have they seen exactly what plans Erdoğan has? They wanted to plant more trees in that park! Yes, they are going to reconstruct the old Ottoman barracks at its centre, but they're going to improve the park around it.'

'If it's going to look so beautiful, what's all this about?'

'About the same thing as usual! Ever since Erdoğan won the first election, in the media here and abroad they've unleashed an unpardonable, totally groundless attack on him. For the past ten years I've been hearing that he's an Islamist, that he's going to introduce sharia law and turn Turkey into another Iran. And no one gives a damn about the fact that nowadays the Turkish economy is a world leader, exports have more than tripled, and that we have three times as many roads and investments, three times as much of everything!

'I started out fifteen years ago with a small kiosk in a rough area, and now I have five shops in various parts of town. I work day and night, but I never complain. And I have what I have largely thanks to the government, which helps small businessmen. And big ones too. It's no accident that the Turkish stock exchange is now the fastest growing in the world.'

'What about Islam? Why do they ban air hostesses from dressing nicely?'

'For goodness sake! If they were such strict Islamists as people say, would I be able to sell alcohol? The whole of eastern Turkey votes for them, those people are very conservative, they think alcohol is worse than the devil, so the government has to make a gesture towards that part of the electorate from time to time. They've been banging on for ages about the fact that when they fly Turkish airlines on a pilgrimage to Mecca they don't want to see an air hostess in a mini-skirt. Is that really so hard to understand?

'But above all our prime minister is so damned pragmatic. And such a capable governor. You didn't want us in the EU? That's your problem. Now we're overtaking Bulgaria and Romania in terms of income and living standards, maybe Greece too. A few more years and the EU will be begging us to join it.'

'But Metin, don't you know that not even China has as many journalists in prison as Turkey? Your prime minister may be the perfect manager, but he really is taking an ever more authoritarian approach. I regard the protests in Gezi Park as a sort of yellow card. As a way of saying: "Prime Minister, don't go down that route".'

'You know what,' says Metin, taking a deep breath, and for a while he stares at the fridge full of alcohol, as if trying to find confirmation in there for the comment he wants to make, 'times are tough the world over. And in times like these I prefer to have a steady hand, even if it's a rough one, running my country. Before Erdoğan, Turkey was in a worse political mess than Italy. Our politicians were incapable of making any decisions; the mafias had enormous influence. Economically we were on a downward slide. Now they've managed to put a stop to all that. And besides' – here Metin pauses and shifts his gaze from the fridge full of alcohol to the door frame and the portrait hanging above it. It's a picture of Mustafa Kemal Atatürk, the father of modern Turkey. There are pictures like it hanging in almost every shop in Turkey, at the barber's, in doctor's surgeries, public offices and restaurants. For the Turks, Atatürk is a saintly figure. 'He ruled in an authoritarian way too,' says Metin at last, and shifts his gaze from the portrait to me.

atatürk's legacy

I'm not surprised it took Metin so long to spit out his comparison of Erdoğan with Atatürk. Although Atatürk died before the Second World War, for the protestors he is still the major reference point. While walking around the edges of the park, I come upon two young men aged about thirty having a heated debate.

'If you're not with us you're not a real Turk,' shouts one. 'You don't care about democracy or development. You don't give a damn about Atatürk's legacy!'

'You're the one who doesn't give a damn about Atatürk!' shouts the other, spoiling for a fight.

Their friends have to come between them, because any moment now, like at a country wedding reception, they're going to start hitting each other in the face. Where Atatürk is concerned there's no joking. Almost everybody in Gezi Park has been quoting him – except perhaps the Kurds (because he blighted their chances of a separate state), the radical left and the anarchists. Even the vegans have a picture of him at their camp – in fact, even the communists have a poster with an equals sign between Atatürk and Lenin.

When the police set about reclaiming Gezi Park, they began by removing the illegal banners with his face on them from the centre that carries his name. As soon as they'd done it, they hung up a new banner, this time a legal one.

'Mustafa Kemal would have occupied Gezi Park with us!' cries a young girl with safety pins stuck in her denim shirt and a ring in her nose. 'It's not about the trees, it's about the Republic!'

In Ankara Prime Minister Erdoğan has devoted several hours to saying very similar things to the Meclis, the Turkish parliament. Except that his words are aimed against those occupying the park.

a few lessons

'Since primary school I've never learned as many things as I have here,' enthuses Metin, who usually works as an accountant at a government office. I'd better not write which one, though they're probably going to fire him anyway. Admittedly, a doctor friend wrote him a sick note for the time of the protests, but the whole thing's too transparent – Metin fell sick on the very day the first tear-gas shells exploded on Taksim Square. In fact his office is entirely dependent on the mayor of Istanbul, Kadir Topbaş, and the mayor is entirely dependent on Prime Minister Erdoğan. It's hard to imagine he would tolerate dissenters who had called for the overthrow of the government among his employees.

'I don't care,' says Metin. To prove it he frowns, and to add spice he smacks his lips, which in Turkey implies disgust. We're sitting outside the green tent which he and his girlfriend have pitched between the canteen, temporarily transformed into Gezi Park's press centre, and the square surrounding a charming fountain. 'The office is dominated by people from the AKP. Over lunch my colleagues in the department talk about who goes to which mosque, and what exactly the prophet Mohammed had in mind when he spoke about women. I'm absolutely serious – that's the sort of thing they discuss. There are a few of us who are non-believers, but until now we've kept quiet. Nobody from my department showed up in Taksim Square. It's better to sit tight and say nothing, because we all know the best job you can have is in the civil service.'

'So what have you learned in Gezi?'

'Lots of things! Do you know for instance how long an excavator keeps burning? You see, you don't know. If it's not put out, it can burn all day, though after a few hours it's mainly just the tyres that are still on fire.

'The prime minister has also forced us to learn how to protect ourselves against tear gas. The masks they're selling here at every turn for three or four lira are best just put on the TV set at home as a souvenir. You'd do better to get a few paper tissues and dampen them with water. And what works best on the gas is lemon or onion.

'You learn a lot about people too. There was a guy coming here every day with his girlfriend. He was a radical, and she looked up to him as if he were a saint. He was calling for the protestors to flood the city and set the US consulate on fire, some cars too, and maybe a shop. And then what? When the police finally came, he was the first to run away before they'd even had time to spray the tear gas. But the girlfriend stayed and coped pretty bravely. She was probably surprised that boyfriend of hers had turned out be such a *yarrak*. What does *yarrak* mean? A male member.'

erdoğan is the darling of the business world

For Sündüz, an Istanbul housewife, the protests in Gezi Park are like science fiction. We are talking in her spacious sitting room in the rich, liberal district of Maçka. Sündüz's husband is a businessman in the textiles industry who travels all over the world, while she spends her time between shopping malls and the equally well-located homes of her friends. Though only a few kilometres from here, Gezi Park seems light years away.

'My children were there and they protested,' says Sündüz. 'My daughter has a beauty salon nearby; she opened it wide for the protestors. They were going there to pee and freshen up. But I've lived half my life in Germany and I have a far more detached view of protests. I don't think anything really awful is likely to happen in Turkey. A mosque? We have a lot of Muslims, so we have mosques as well. People keep wailing that more and more women are wearing headscarves. But it's not true. The research shows that the number is falling. It's just that those who do wear them go out of the house more often nowadays. That has to be a good thing, doesn't it? If they sit at home, their husbands will beat them. Better for them to go out.'

'What about the prime minister's authoritarian aspirations? And the tear gas?'

'Quite, the tear gas. Listen – the prime minister used tear gas and there's a fuss all over the world. T-E-A-R G-A-S! Not weapons, not troops. Not a single tank went out, a riot control unit just came along and imposed order, just as it would have done anywhere else in Europe. I've seen this sort of police operation in Germany lots of times as well, and there was no global hysteria about it, or comparisons with Middle Eastern despots.

'If it were Mubarak, he'd have fired live ammunition. If it were Assad, he'd have razed half the country to the ground. But Erdoğan used tear gas, just as the police in Paris or Berlin do. So what if he doesn't always come running at the bidding of others? Was Margaret Thatcher any different? Or Jacques Chirac? If the young people in EU countries think they could occupy a major city centre without getting any tear gas, they must be clueless about Europe. These days Turkey is far more European than many people realise. More than Erdoğan himself realises. Of course I can see he has authoritarian tendencies; maybe he really does believe he's a sultan. But on the other hand, the EU is the main partner for Turkish businessmen. And Erdoğan is the darling of the business world. He can shout and rage, but he's never going to do anything against the interests of the people who bring in the money.'

the purgatory of istanbul

THEY GET UP while the city is still at play. They put on dark-blue trousers, lace-up boots and T-shirts with the emblem of the city that employs them. They take life-saving kits, basic medicines and warm clothing.

They also take a supply of large plastic bags.

A Honda jeep takes them to the beaches. Metre by metre, they comb them, first the most highly frequented ones, then the less popular ones. They are looking for the remains of boats, shoes, sweaters, backpacks, hats, upside-down dinghies, sodden blankets, documents, passports and children's bootees – anything the sea may have cast up. But first and foremost they are looking for bodies.

'Five years ago the sea cast up two Africans on the beach, right next to the luxury hotels, and some tourists found them,' says Kazım, one of the men in dark-blue trousers and lace-up boots. 'Tourists don't like finding corpses. The British, Germans or Poles come here for a holiday and they pay a lot for it. We've got to do the cleaning before they get up.'

special offer

We're sitting in a small café in the market area of Istanbul. Half a kilometre away from us is the famous Topkapı Palace, the residence of the Ottoman sultans. Day after day thousands of tourists come and see where that lucky devil the sultan ate, where he slept and where he kept his harem full of beautiful women.

But none of that concerns Mahmud, an Iraqi with a greying beard and nicotine-stained fingers. He smokes a cigarette every five minutes, regular as clockwork, right down to the filter, until it starts to burn his fingers.

Five years ago he was working as an interpreter for the Americans, until their enemies passed a death sentence on him. The Americans couldn't or wouldn't help him.

'There is an aid programme for former interpreters, but Allah alone knows why it didn't include me,' he says. 'Two of my colleagues were killed, so there was no point in waiting any longer. I took my wife and five-year-old daughter, and we fled.'

Oruç Ulusoy, a lawyer from Izmir who helps immigrants, warns me: 'Don't believe their stories. They don't tell the truth. For them the truth is too dangerous.'

But Mahmud's British accent adds to his credibility. He says a cousin sent him 1,000 euros from Germany, and his family in Iraq saved up the same amount again. It was enough to get them to Istanbul by transporter lorry.

'I sent my wife and child off to Greece,' he says. 'The first boat was turned back by the coastguards. The second started taking on water, and they only just managed to get back to shore.'

If Mahmud is to be believed, the third time they made the voyage successfully.

'It's a good thing it was a success, because a *kaçakçı*, or smuggler, takes the money for three attempts. It's a special offer, like in the supermarket. But if you don't get there the third time, you've got to save up all over again,' says Mahmud.

His wife is now in Munich, but Mahmud is stuck in Istanbul. He knows everyone here, from the petty conmen, via the pimps, to the smugglers. Thanks to him I can find out a great deal.

Mahmud needs to save up 2,000 euros. He teaches English, he helps to sell stolen passports and brings in customers for the smugglers. He doesn't earn a fortune, but if it goes well, in a year's time he'll be in Germany. Right now, money is what matters most to Mahmud, so when I say: 'I want you to help me find Yusuf,' Mahmud doesn't ask who Yusuf is or why I'm looking for him. He just asks: 'How much will you pay me?'

I can't pay him. So he spreads his hands, stubs out the cigarette he has smoked right down to the filter, and goes on his way.

bridge

There are two Istanbuls.

The first one belongs to the tourists, five-star hotels and party-goers. This is where Orhan Pamuk seeks the sources of his nostalgia, while Japanese visitors draped in cameras photograph every millimetre of it. Each year over ten million tourists come here, with over thirty million visiting the country as a whole. Almost ten per cent of the Turkish budget comes out of their pockets.

But it isn't just tourists who love Turkey. In recent years it has been a paradise for businessmen attracted by economic growth of more than seven per cent, and also for the politicians who are taking notice of its efforts to reconcile Europe and Asia.

The moustachioed prime minister Erdoğan describes this Istanbul and this sort of Turkey as a bridge between East and West.

But these days the real bridge is the other Istanbul. To see it, you have to step off the tourist trail and into the side streets, and then sharpen your vision.

Then you can see the Africans using the last of their energy to pull carts laden with scrap metal, the Chinese slicing cucumbers for kebabs in a basement, or the Indians selling fake perfume, with bags under their eyes that have stuck to their faces for good. They put up with this dog's life because they're dreaming about Europe. They believe our wealth – and from their point of view Poland is a super-rich country too – is the answer to all their problems.

These people are stuck on the bridge the Turkish prime minister talks about. Nobody even attempts to add up how many of them are living here. The experts speculate that each year from 500,000 to two million immigrants pass through the purgatory of Istanbul.

'We worked in a factory on sixteen-hour shifts,' a refugee from China was quoted in the Istanbul press. 'The owner gave us accommodation in a shed behind the factory. For eighteen people we had four beds and one chair. After three months he threw us out without paying us. However, even worse than the fact that he didn't pay us, is that ever since we've been living on a rubbish dump.'

yusuf

I met Yusuf seven years ago at a small class C hotel in Istanbul. He was the same age as I was, with long hair tied in a ponytail and a beard, which made him look like an Arab version of the Polish blues-rock musician Rysiek Riedel. He too had just one dream – to get to Europe.

He had come from Libya (on a tourist visa to Syria, and from there with the smugglers). This surprised me, because the smugglers also sail from Libya to Italy, which would have worked out cheaper for him.

'I'm afraid of water,' said Yusuf shamefully.

He had good reason to be ashamed. He should have boarded the first boat, he explained, and either died or sailed across, instead of which he had wasted time and his father's money.

He'd give his right arm for his family.

'But I had to leave,' he stressed, his gaze fixed on the Bosporus separating Europe and Asia. 'To have a wife, you've got to be able to support her. In Libya I was a teacher, and I couldn't even support myself.'

However, Yusuf wasn't good at being serious for long, and he immediately changed the subject. He started asking me questions about Polish girls, films and wages. Whatever answer I gave, his eyes lit up like the ships' lamps on the Bosporus. Then he calculated how long he'd have to work in his country to get a Polish salary, and whistled in appreciation.

My pal Yusuf was a really good friend. When his money ran out, the hotel owner offered him a job on the night shift. Every time I went to Istanbul I would drop in there for a cup of coffee.

'Istanbul is an incredible city,' he said. 'Here you'll find the sort of people who'll share their last crust of bread with you, as well as the sort who'll cut out your kidneys and dump you in the canal.'

He was looking for the first kind; I hope he found them, because a year ago he sent me an e-mail saying: 'I'm learning to swim :-)'.

I asked: 'Are you moving on?' Again he replied: ':-)'.

Since then he hadn't been in touch again. One day he had simply upped and left the class C hotel, where he had been working for almost seven years.

mahmud

Two days after my conversation with Mahmud the receptionist wakes me up. Abdullah is waiting in the lobby, a petty conman who tried to sell me a lump of hashish a few days earlier. He has a message from Mahmud: 'Let's meet at noon, same café as last time.'

I arrive a quarter of an hour early.

'What's your newspaper's print-run?' asks Mahmud.

'Half a million,' I say.

Mahmud quickly does some calculations.

'I'll help you,' he says at last. 'But you'll have to do something for me too. What? You'll find out in due course. But now we're going on a tour of the city.'

So we finish our coffee and head off. We start with Eminönü, the ferry terminus from which for one-and-a-half lira (about fifty pence) you can sail to the other side of the Bosporus, to Asia. The Yeni Cami Mosque is located here. Behind it the market begins, and in front of it there is a square.

'The thieves in this square specialise in passports,' says Mahmud.

Then he explains that the market in passports is as up and down as the Turkish stock exchange. Five years ago a Polish passport was only worth as much as a Tajik one, in other words nothing. But since then we've got into the EU, followed by Schengen, so today the immigrants have to pay 1,000 or even 1,500 dollars for a small book with an eagle stamped on it.

The most expensive passports of all are German and Italian – more than 2,000 dollars each. Iranian ones sell pretty well too. They are easily available – because Iran is Turkey's neighbour – and they provide entry into Bosnia. From Bosnia to Italy is only a stone's throw, and every Libyan has relatives or friends in Italy.

'Oh, look at that!' says Mahmud, pointing out a grey-haired man who looks like an American, around whom a crowd of people has suddenly gathered. 'The Kurds are setting a trap,' says Mahmud. 'They're brilliant at it. They'll even get your passport out of your underpants.' And although this time the American seems to have got away with it, Mahmud still nods in admiration.

Two days later two Kurds try to rob me too, this time of my cash. My photographer, my interpreter and I catch one of them and hand him over to the police. I spend half a day at the police station to make a statement, during which time eight people come in to report the theft of their passports. Sixteen more show up at the tourist police office. In a single day, just around Eminönü Square, Dutch, Australian and German passports and one Norwegian passport have all gone missing.

'A thief often has an order for a particular passport,' one of the officers tells me. 'Sometimes he'll follow a tourist for a day or more. They call you "passport donors".'

I ask Mahmud what can be done with a Polish passport issued in my name.

'Most often they're falsified – it's easier to swap a single page than fake an entire passport. But sometimes someone buys them without any changes. People on the move are so keen to get out of here that they'll believe anything – even that you can be black and enter Europe with a photo of a white man called Szabłowski in your passport.'

the shipwreck

In September 2003 the sea cast the bodies of twenty-four immigrants onto the Turkish shore, most likely from Pakistan. The Turks were shocked – it was the biggest tragedy on their seas for many years.

Meanwhile it was just a harbinger of things to come. Only three months later sixty people were drowned on their way to Rhodes. They included Iraqis, Afghans and Jordanians, as well as a woman and her ten-year-old daughter.

Following this disaster some of the resorts started to employ the people in dark-blue trousers who look for bodies to make sure the tourists won't find them.

The next day, a ferry on its way to Rhodes rescued one single man, a twenty-year-old refugee from Iraq who by a miracle had clung onto a piece of driftwood.

For a month all the Turkish media did interviews with him. He was on the front pages of the newspapers, and the charitable organisations vied with one another to arrange asylum, a flat and a job for him. Even people on the move, who were also very poor, collected money to help him.

'I already knew that boy from Iraq. Allah gave him a second life,' says Mahmud. 'As if his mother had given birth to him all over again. And do you know what he's done with his new life?'

Mahmud leads me down the backstreets of Taksim, Istanbul's red light and party district. In a small street where the transvestites have their rendezvous, sits a balding young man with a tufty red beard. He is staring at the road, smiling and muttering to himself. A trickle of saliva has congealed on his chin.

'You're stoned again! Bloody hell, you're stoned again!' screams Mahmud, and grabs at the boy. Then he looks at me, and at the boy again. 'He couldn't hold out,' he says. 'He couldn't hold out,' he repeats, and it is a short while before he lets go of the boy's sweater – the young man to whom Allah gave a second life, if that really was the same person. I have no way of checking.

surfers

Once the immigrants have passed through the purgatory of Istanbul, they set off for the seaside. Hidden in transporter lorries and in car boots they reach Basmane, a district of Izmir.

Once again their route crosses the tourist route; Izmir is the Turkish Los Angeles, a beautiful port with an old castle and excellent food. The tourists head for Basmane too – this is where the cheapest hotels are located. Ours is called the Şükran. Right on the doorstep we pass three Africans, who are nibbling sunflower seeds and watching the weather channel so intently that it looks as if you could improve it simply by staring.

The bazaar in Basmane is probably the only bazaar in the world that starts up at around midnight. Here they sell bananas, oranges, watermelons, fresh bread, sausages, hard-boiled eggs, chocolate and energy drinks. A few of the shops even have ropes, clasp knives and life jackets on offer – everything that might come in handy during the crossing.

The place is crowded with people. They're haggling, laughing and shoving things into small backpacks (as with airlines, you pay the smugglers through the nose for excess baggage; the price only includes a small backpack).

Round the corner there's an internet café and some cheap phones. Burkina Faso – one euro per minute. Afghanistan – eighty cents. Syria – sixty. Now and then a fleeting figure dashes past to tell the family he's already in Izmir; only a short boat ride to go, and he'll be in the world of his dreams – Europe.

Fifty kilometres from Basmane lies Çeşme, the very last port before the EU border. In the season this is paradise for windsurfers. When the wind is blowing from Greece, they throw their boards onto the water and ride the crests of the waves. The wind from Greece comes down from the mountains, and can pick up a lot of speed. While it is blowing, the people on the move must sit and wait; a boat has to have a good motor to sail against the wind, and a boat with a good motor costs more. So the people on the move have the time to call their families, buy some chocolate, chat with their pals, or nibble sunflower seeds.

Until along comes the wind they're waiting for from inland. Then the windsurfers head for the bar or the disco, or go on a tour of ancient Ephesus.

Cars drive down to the beaches bordering the city. From these same beaches where the surfers were living it up during the day, now the smugglers' boats are setting off. The immigrants I spoke to in Izmir had mentioned that you can often hear a disco in the background.

'I couldn't believe they were having a good time there. I was thinking I might get killed very soon, and they're having a disco!' said Malcolm from Eritrea. 'But then I realised it was a good thing, because the engine was making a very loud noise – if it weren't for the disco, anyone could have heard us.'

mosque

I don't want to stand out of the crowd in Basmane, so I sit in the street and pretend to be asleep, as if I've nothing to do with what's going on around there. They might take me for a druggie, or maybe for one of the people on the move. 'As long as they don't take me for a journalist,' I think, disguising myself as best I can.

Unnecessarily – business is conducted quite openly. Today the wind happens to be blowing in the right direction, so now and then the door of one of the small, cheap hotels opens and dark figures get into taxis, vans and even a vehicle marked 'furniture'. Now and then a police car drives past, but the policemen don't even slow down.

The hotels here are called: 'Europe', 'Lovely Journey', 'Friend' and 'Dream'. There's a *nazarlık* hanging in every doorway – a bright blue amulet with a black eye, which is meant to protect travellers from bad luck.

At the corner the hotel owners have established a small mosque. You can drop in there at any time to remind Allah of your existence before your journey.

Behind the mosque there is another cluster of telephones. I get talking to two lads from Nigeria, Omar and Nnamdi. They both look about twenty years old.

'We're going in two hours, when the first cars come back. I called to tell my mother,' says Omar happily.

'Are we afraid? Brother, God is great and everything will be as He decides,' says Nnamdi, clapping me on the shoulder, and they run off to the bazaar to do their last-minute shopping.

For a while I stand by a shop selling fresh bread.

'Are you sailing too?' asks the salesman.

'No, not today,' I reply.

'If you want to buy a ticket, you can come to me,' he says, and winks.

kaçakçı

In autumn and winter the hotels and restaurants on the coast give tourists a thirty-per cent discount. As everyone knows, the weather is worse, and you can't go sailing. But for all that, there's peace and quiet, and the beauty of nature.

The *kaçakçı*, or smugglers, give a thirty-per cent discount too. As everyone knows, a body that falls into the water will cool down much faster than in summer. Death is instantaneous. But there are pluses too: in winter the Greeks are less vigilant about guarding the border.

'Once the *kaçakçı* used to smuggle cigarettes, alcohol and other things,' I read in the work of Professor İçduygu, a leading expert on migration. 'Now they've switched to people. There's no great big mafia here with a godfather in charge. The structure is more like al-Qaida: lots of small groups which cooperate, but are independent. Nevertheless they are capable of organising a complex journey from Kabul to London.'

The professor ran a survey among smugglers who are in prison. According to his research none of them thinks he is doing anything reprehensible. More than that – they reckon they're doing a lot to help people, and that their work is a sort of mission.

In the small towns and villages people know who is a *kaçakçı*. The fishermen in Ayvalık– a charming old port not far from ancient Pergamon – pointed one of them out to me. They call him Ahmet Baba, meaning Father Ahmet. A small man in an oversized coat, with a fag-end glued to his ashen lips, he looked a bit like a cartoon character. He had come to the harbour to buy fish. Two heavies came trailing along in his wake, Uzbeks or Tajiks at a guess.

Ahmet Baba works for Kurbağa – the Frog. Kurbağa and his men have a monopoly on smuggling people from the Ayvalık area to Lesbos. In the season, never a day goes by without their boats sailing from the neighbouring villages.

'If there's a good wind, at dawn every now and then you hear *prr, prr, prr*,' says Ismail, a fisherman from Ayvalık. 'It's their motors. Then we usually say: "*Kurbağa geldi*", meaning "There goes the Frog".'

Ahmet Baba looks like a kindly uncle. He greets everyone jovially, gives high fives and kisses his old friends on both cheeks. As he walks past me, we almost bump shoulders. He gives me a friendly smile, like a person who is happy and wishes others well too.

He knows I'm looking for information on the *kaçakçı*. He must know – it's my third day in Ayvalık by now, and Ahmet Baba knows everything. Even so, he asks in a genial tone: 'Are you a tourist?'

'Yes,' I misinform him. 'What about you?'

'Me? I'm the local oddball,' he says, laughing, and walks off. His heavies are laughing too, and it's making their large bellies wobble.

fishermen

In September 2008 Ahmet Baba sent out some dinghies from Behramkale. From here it is only five kilometres in a straight line to the Greek coast.

In the year 347BC Behramkale was called Assos. Aristotle came here to restore his frazzled nerves when he wasn't chosen to succeed Plato at the famous Athenian Academy. From the local harbour he would make trips to examine the flora and fauna of the island of Lesbos.

Ahmet's boats were bound for Lesbos too, setting off less than a kilometre away from the harbour where Aristotle started his journeys centuries ago. It all went fairly efficiently, until at about 2am a boat appeared carrying Greek border guards.

From the unguarded beach near Behramkale the whole scene was clearly visible. Ahmet Baba quickly took to his heels, but four dinghies the size of cockle shells, which had already managed to sail out into Greek territorial waters, were left at sea, with thirty-eight people on board.

The Greeks acted aggressively, making big waves with their motorboat, and one of the dinghies capsized, tossing people into the sea. To make them get out of the water faster, the border guards chivvied them by firing shots.

Then they threw a rope, towed all four cockle shells back into Turkish territorial waters and took away their oars and motors, condemning the passengers to drift, which could have been the death of them.

'Dammit all!' cursed Ismail the fisherman. He is one of the very few who have bigger vessels in which they can sail out for tuna. But that day, as soon as he and his brother-in-law (who works with him) set off from the port, they saw the four dinghies full of people calling for help. They had no oars, and the weather was getting worse and worse.

The fishermen picked up the refugees and took them to the coastguard's station. Now Ismail isn't sure he did the right thing.

'First I was accused of aiding the smugglers,' he tells me. 'I had to go and explain myself. Finally the prosecutor said: "I haven't found anything but I'll be keeping an eye on you".'

The fishermen here have often helped immigrants.

'In summer there are problems almost every day,' says Ismail, and his brother-in-law agrees. 'The Greeks shoot at them. Sometimes they make holes in the boats, and before he can start fishing, a fisherman spends two hours sailing about picking up those people so they won't drown.'

'We make our living by catching fish,' adds the brother-in-law. 'When we hauled that lot out, we couldn't work for the next two weeks – first we had to make statements, then we had to be fingerprinted. How am I supposed to help those people if my wife's got nothing to give the children to eat afterwards?'

Ismail continues: 'Now we're afraid to help. What's more, there are so many of those dinghies now that it's impossible to help them all anyway. Am I sorry I helped them that time? Bloody hell, yes, I am. I have to say I regret it.'

border guards

In December 2007 thirty-one bodies were found near a town called Seferihisar. Nobody knows how many people drowned that time. According to three men who were rescued, the boat had taken more than seventy immigrants on board.

In March 2008 at least four people drowned near the city of Hatay. A week later, six more died near a place called Didim. In October seventeen bodies were found by the coast guards not far from Çanakkale – right next to ancient Troy. While I was working on this chapter, two bodies were found near Ayvalık, and two more in the Bodrum area.

In November 2008 Human Rights Watch accused Greece of illegally sending refugees back to Turkey, while the Turks were accused of keeping asylum seekers in inhuman conditions.

At the same time a German organisation called Pro Asyl published a report on the Turkish-Greek coast, sub-titled 'The truth may be bitter, but it must be told!' – a piece of graffiti from the wall of a detention centre on Lesbos.

According to Karl Kopp, one of the authors of the report: 'We talked to immigrants, fishermen and people who work for human rights organisations. It turned out the Greek border guards often beat up, and even shoot at immigrants. They turn people who sail into their waters back to Turkey and leave them to their fate. Anyone who does nevertheless succeed in getting across to Greece ends up at an immigrant detention centre where he might spend many months in very poor conditions.'

attractions

Some young Greeks helped with both reports. The facts they discovered made a huge impression on many of them, inspiring them to produce a special leaflet.

Don't miss our special offer!
Our officers will guarantee you some unforgettable attractions!
They'll welcome you by firing at your boat.
Then they'll make some lovely big waves so you'll capsize.
If you don't capsize they'll throw you a rope and tow you to a survival course on one of our desert islands.
If by some miracle you still manage to sail across to Greece, there's another attraction waiting for you – massage with truncheons, followed by a few years at an attractive detention centre.
Fancy a walk? You'll get one as often as once a week!
Welcome to Greece! You'll enjoy yourself to death!

The picture is like something out of a tourist brochure – there's a beach, some palm trees and a nice little yacht, but instead of the usual skimpily dressed females, standing against the background of this scene there's a man in handcuffs.

The young Greeks have distributed these leaflets around all the beaches, bars and discos on the islands bordering Turkey.

We find one on the ferry from Ayvalık to Lesbos. The crossing takes an hour and a half. The captain says he often sees boats full of immigrants.

'In summer I sometimes see more than a dozen at once. We make our return trip at six in the morning, when the ones who sailed out at night are just coming in. Though once I saw a dinghy full of immigrants sailing into the main port of Lesbos right in the middle of the day. Those guys had some nerve!'

icarus

Dedalus was a brilliant inventor. When the tyrant Minos imprisoned him on Crete, he made wings out of bird feathers, took off into the air with his son Icarus, and escaped.

We know what happened next: Icarus flew too high and the wax holding the feathers together began to melt. He plummeted headlong, crashed to the rocks and drowned.

A few centuries later Pieter Brueghel painted *The Fall of Icarus*. A fine ship is coming into port, a farmer is ploughing his field, a shepherd is tending his sheep, and far in the distance we can see the leg of the drowning Icarus and a few remaining feathers. As Tadeusz Różewicz wrote about this painting:

> *the venture of Icarus is not their venture*
> *this is how it must end*
> *And there is nothing*
> *earth-shaking*
> *about a beautiful ship sailing on*
> *to its port of destination*[*]

---

[*] 'A Didactic Tale: V, Rights and Duties', in *'The Survivor' and Other Poems*, translated by Magnus J. Krynski and Robert A. Maguire, Princeton University Press, 1976.

Andrea, a banker from Athens, has stuck a copy of Brueghel's picture on her fridge. She also collects poems and stories about Icarus. What about Różewicz's poem?

'It's lovely, but it's not true. In the global village there's no such thing as "not our venture",' she says. And then rather poetically adds: 'Nowadays too the Icaruses dream they can fly off to a better life. Here, on this coast, their dreams are shattered on the rocks. And the Icarus from the myth drowned... fifty kilometres from here, off the island of Ikaria.'

Two years ago Andrea moved from Athens to the island of Lesbos.

'The first day I went out for a drive. Outside the city I saw a woman with a baby wrapped in a blanket. I gave her and her friend a lift into town. They had just arrived on a boat from Turkey and had arranged to meet another smuggler at the port.'

It turned out women of this kind are an everyday sight on Lesbos. In the season not a day passes without groups of immigrants walking through the very centre of Mytilene, the island's capital. Each year thousands of them make their way through here. In the local cemetery there are now more than a hundred gravestones marked 'Unknown immigrant'. These are the ones cast up by the sea.

'Most of them already have onward transport arranged,' says Andrea. 'But some of them have nothing, and some fall into the clutches of our public services.'

To help the immigrants, Andrea and her friends have founded an 'Icaruses' society. In summer, when the largest number of them are trying to get to Greece, they drive around the coast distributing clothes and blankets, providing information about the rights to which they are entitled, and offering a lawyer, a doctor and an interpreter.

'All this should be guaranteed to them by our government,' says Andrea. 'But the government doesn't give a damn.'

As we are talking in a local bar, two women and two men pass before our eyes. They are soaking wet and look dreadfully tired. One of the women is wearing a headscarf. The other has her head uncovered, but seems completely absent, as if she doesn't understand where she has ended up and why.

'She looks ill, or as if she has had a terrible experience,' says Andrea.

Each of them is carrying a small backpack. The men, in jeans and striped shirts, are looking around nervously. We run up to them, and Andrea asks if they need help.

The immigrants are terrified.

'Please don't talk to us. Please don't look at us,' says the older of the men. 'In two hours we won't be here. I beg you, dear madam, dear sir, please don't take any notice of us at all.'

dinghies

None of the immigrants we met would agree to have their photo taken. So the photographer and I drive along the unguarded beaches around Çeşme and Ayvalık, and then the stony coast of the island of Lesbos. Kazım – the man in dark-blue trousers and lace-up boots who looks for bodies – tells us which beaches he and his workmates don't go to. We make a tour of all of them.

In various places we find punctured rubber dinghies cast up on shore, five in all. One of them, not far from Çeşme, has some clothes floating around it too – a jacket, hat and flip-flops.

We call the police.

'Oh, someone must have thrown them away,' they trivialise the matter. 'People throw things in the sea instead of taking them to the dump.'

According to Oruç Ulusoy, the lawyer who helps immigrants in Izmir: 'In this part of the world even a baseball cap cast up on the shore represents somebody's tragedy. Unfortunately our police continue to regard it as the EU's problem, not theirs.'

what I think of you

Mahmud never found Yusuf. He did hear something about a Libyan who worked at a hotel, but whether it was Yusuf and what happened to him next, he doesn't know.

We're having coffee together again, not at the café this time but at an electrical goods shop which Mahmud sometimes looks after for the friend who owns it.

'I've got mixed up in some bad business,' he tells me quite unexpectedly. 'I didn't go to college just to end up dealing in stolen passports. I was meant to be a respectable interpreter and teacher, maybe even an academic. But when I was your age, the war came, and then emigration. And by now I'm done for.'

For a while we remain silent, because I don't know how to respond to such an unexpected confession. This silence seems to irritate Mahmud.

'Did you know that the biggest number of immigrants in Turkey nowadays are Iraqis?' he finally asks. It's true. Since the war began, more than five million of his compatriots have fled the country. 'You Poles, British and Americans have made it impossible to live in my country. And now you shut your doors in our faces. Is this the famous democracy you're so keen to promote?' he asks, getting more and more annoyed.

I don't really know what to say, so I sit quietly. Mahmud calms down. He takes a piece of paper out of his shirt pocket.

'Now I'll tell you how you can repay me. When you write your article, you'll include my appeal. It's short.'

And he reads out: 'I, Mahmud X., former interpreter for the American army, have a big favour to ask Western Europe.

Send an army unit here to castrate the lot of us. We've got nothing to feed our children anyway. And when we try to come to your country to get an honest job, you shoot at us and drive us away.

'Castrate us. You'll be doing us a service, as well as yourselves.'

it's out of love, sister

1

HATICE SHIELDS HER MOUTH with her hand, as if she's afraid the words will spill out of her. She doesn't want to talk. She has never spoken to anyone about those matters, and she never intended to.

I explain that she's not in any danger, but it's not about danger. Hatice simply doesn't know how to talk about what she went through.

For what can she say about her father? Fathers love their daughters the world over. Hatice's father wanted to kill her.

And what can she say about her mother? A mother should protect her daughter with her own body, but Hatice's mother shouted at her husband: 'When are you finally going to kill that whore?'

What can she say about her brother, who came to her house with a knife? Or her sister, with whom she had slept in the same bed since childhood, but who didn't warn her?

If her husband Ahmet weren't a strong person, Hatice wouldn't be alive now.

We meet at their house. We agree that if they find it impossible to talk, I won't insist.

Hatice receives me wearing harem pants with an oriental pattern and a headscarf that entirely conceals her hair. Ahmet has a bushy moustache and a checked flannel shirt. They are both twenty-two, and have been together for five years. The marriage, like most in their village, was arranged, but they're very happy.

Their flat consists of two chairs, a sofa bed and a rug on the wall. They haven't yet acquired more. They haven't any children. They live near the market, where you can buy pistachios, watermelons, cheese and bread. Ahmet works there, selling honey. They have some friends, and they've started a new life.

The old one ended four years ago, when Ahmet went into the army. In the meantime, Hatice was to go and live with his aunt. The aunt is a widow who lives with her son, so it was ideal. In eastern Turkey a woman should not live on her own – that would be immoral.

The problem was that the day after Ahmet left, his aunt's second son, Abdullah, knocked at Hatice's door. He shouldn't have done that. Hatice told him to go away.

He went, but the next day he came back, and started tugging at the door handle. 'Open up, I'm going to deal with you!' he shouted.

Hatice stood frozen to the spot. She didn't know what to do. Shout? Abdullah would play the innocent. He wouldn't come clean. Tell the aunt? For Allah's sake! No one would believe a woman!

So Hatice held the door shut with all her might and Abdullah gave up. But the next day he decided to take revenge.

2

From above, Diyarbakır looks like a pancake with a few blisters of air bulging up on its surface. In places there are some dark brown bumps protruding. As the plane descends, I can see that they're rocks, scattered here as if they had sprung out of the ground.

At the edge of this plain are the blue threads of the Tigris and the Euphrates, which marked the borders of ancient Mesopotamia. This is where the first civilisation was founded. Here the ancients sought the ruins of the Biblical Eden. The patriarchs Abraham and Noah were born very near here.

The issues that concern us probably go back to those days. You enter the city through a wall of black brick, built by the Byzantines over a thousand years ago. According to the guidebook, after the Great Wall of China, this is the second most famous wall in the world. There should be thousands of tourists coming here, but there aren't. Diyarbakır has a bad reputation. It is the capital of a country that doesn't exist – Kurdistan – and of a people who are prepared to take up arms and fight for its right to exist.

Only a few years ago big business used to bypass this city, but since the Kurds have ceased to plant bombs and the army has stopped shelling the neighbouring villages, businessmen have been coming here too. Diyarbakır has a million inhabitants. These days no city in Europe would be ashamed of its main drag, which has modern shops and expensive restaurants. Every month there are more and more of them, because the devil known as consumerism has settled in for good.

Only the old men with the beards of patriarchs take no part in all this. They sit in the shade of the trees outside the mosques and complain. They don't like television, mobile phones, jeans, short skirts, schools or newspapers. They don't like anything that brings confusion into their lives, or anything that tries to change their age-old principles.

3

Each year in eastern Turkey a few dozen young women are killed. One after another they die in strange or unknown circumstances. They are the victims of honour killing, a tradition that bids the relatives to kill women who stain the family honour.

Ayşe Gökkan, a journalist for Kurdish television, is writing a book about honour killing. 'The culture here is based on male dominance. Any resistance should be punished,' she says.

According to Ayşe Figen Zeybek who represents Kamer, an organisation that tries to prevent violence within the family: 'This tradition is several thousand years old. It is unwritten and very fluid. Sometimes even marital infidelity can be forgiven. Another time a girl dies because she wants to wear jeans.'

'Sorry?'

'Girls are killed because they want to be independent. In recent years poverty has driven many families out of the villages into Diyarbakır. It's often as if they have come here from the Middle Ages. It's an immense shock, especially for the young girls.'

'Meaning?'

'They find themselves in the middle of a global village – mobile phones, the internet, MTV. They see their peers who can go out of the house without a man to mind them, who can dress nicely instead of wearing a headscarf and harem pants all the time, or who have boyfriends before getting married. And they want to live like them.

'Meanwhile, their fathers are bewildered too. Keeping watch over their daughters was easy back in their villages. But in the city, Allah knows what might enter a girl's head. And instead of sitting at home like her mother, grandmother and great-grandmother, the daughter comes and says: "I want to go to the cinema, I want to go for a walk, I want new shoes". It is usually the finest girls who are killed, the bravest and most out-going.'

On the day I was admiring Mesopotamia from the plane, a father killed his daughter in Şanurfia. Why? Because she sent a text message to a radio station with best wishes for her boyfriend. Her first name and surname were mentioned on air. The father believed she had tarnished her virginity.

Two weeks earlier in the town of Silvan a husband killed his wife. He told the family that at the time of their wedding she was not a virgin. Her parents reckoned he must have been right.

4

While Abdullah was banging on Hatice's door, a hundred kilometres away another drama was taking place. In the village of Yalım not far from Mardin – a lovely, ancient fortress – thirty-five-year-old Şemse Allak was raped by a fifty-five-year-old man.

People say Şemse was a bit mad. A shopkeeper from Mardin says plainly that she was retarded.

But it might be to do with a different form of madness. A weaving teacher who knew her says Şemse didn't want to get married, and that was why people from the village regarded her as a lunatic.

The rapist was called Halil Acil. He had a wife and two children. He lived on the outskirts of the village. Beyond his grey stone house the fields began, dotted with hundreds of rocks.

Şemse lived nearer the centre with her father, mother and brothers, by the road that leads to the mosque. Every day, on her way back from the fields along the road, which climbs gently up hill, she would pass Halil's house. Evil tongues say that Halil didn't rape her at all, but that they had been sleeping together for ages, and that Şemse made up the fairy tale about being raped when it turned out she was pregnant. Apart from gossip there is nothing to imply that this was in fact the case – neither the police inquiry nor that of the women's organisations.

Nobody knows if Halil found Şemse attractive. Some say he had been in love with her for ages. Others say he took advantage of her in the hope of getting away with it, because even if Şemse told someone about the rape, nobody would believe a madwoman.

When Şemse fell pregnant, her family came to Halil and said: 'You've got to marry her, or else we'll kill you and her too'. The man already had a wife, but the family was suggesting marriage before an imam. You can only marry one woman before a state official, but before a servant of God you can marry two or three.

Halil was willing to agree, but in addition Şemse's family demanded several thousand Turkish lira. Halil didn't have that much, so the woman's brothers went away with nothing.

But both they and Halil knew this wasn't the end. A loving family always defends the honour of its daughters.

5

The origins of honour killing are impossible to determine, but they are probably descended from nomadic tribal traditions. A father could get a dowry for a girl as long as she was a virgin. If she wasn't, the husband would send her back. It wasn't just that she had brought shame on her family, but she would have to be maintained by it for the rest of her life. For nomads the number of people needing to be fed was of enormous significance, as was the money brought in by a dowry. According to the scholars, that was probably the reason why the nomads started killing their daughters.

They also killed women who wanted to divorce – in this case the dowry had to be returned. And they killed those who refused to agree to a marriage arranged by the family.

According to Ayşe Figen Zeybek from the Kamer organisation: 'The tragic death of Şemse Allak moved the whole country. At her graveside we rather blatantly publicised our programme. We guarantee survival for any woman who comes forward to us.'

'And how's it going?'

'Since 2003 we have saved over 150 girls. If a girl's family is determined to kill her, we find a refuge for her in another city. We send her there and help her to start a new life. The refuges are closely guarded, because some families will invest major resources in this. Two years ago the daughter of one of the heads of a big family ran off with a boyfriend. They sent twenty cars after her, and searched for her in all the big cities. They found her, but she escaped her killer by climbing through a window, and now nobody knows what's happened to her.'

'How do you know if a family is determined to kill?'

'A psychologist goes with us. He judges whether they can be trusted if they promise not to kill.'

'Do they make that promise?'

'It's a tricky process. You can't just go to the house and say: "Apparently you're planning to kill your daughter. I'd advise you not to!" First we gather information. If the family is religious, we go with an imam. If the father works at a factory, we ask the manager for support. Once a doctor helped us who had treated the grandmother. Another time a government minister called from Ankara who was related to one of the families. All these people explain: "There's no need to kill! There are lots of other solutions!"'

'What do the families say to that?'

'A few days ago I was in Viranşehir, a small village outside Şanlıurfa. The family had told the girl to kill herself. An uncle was sending her text messages saying: "Kill yourself or you'll die in torment". Why? Because she had a boyfriend at school, and he had given her a lift in his car. In the countryside that's unthinkable.'

'And then what?'

'It always feels strange having to bargain with a family for the life of their own daughter. But I've got my own special tricks by now. I explain that I'm from there as well, and that my daughter has a boyfriend too, but I have no intention of killing her for that reason. I show them photos on my phone. I say she's good at maths, but has trouble with Turkish. This time the father caught on. He started complaining that his daughter has to study Turkish, and that the school's to blame for everything that's wrong, because what's the point of Kurds learning Turkish?

'I always try to rouse the dormant parent in them. I ask how much their daughter weighed at birth, what illnesses she had as a child, and what was the first word she said – Mummy or Daddy? If I can rouse the parents, we're on the straight.'

'And this time? Did it work?'

'They promised not to do anything to her. The daughter swore she'd always come home from school with her older brother from now on. Though it's a risk. Last year we had the famous case of Ayşegül Alpaslan. This woman's husband promised, in the presence of the police, never to hit her again. A week later he beat her to death.'

6

So what is honour? This was the question put to some inhabitants of eastern Turkey by Professor Yakın Ertürk, who worked with a group of volunteers to write a report for the United Nations Development Programme (UNDP). The report, entitled *The Dynamics of Honour Killings in Turkey*, is the most comprehensive study on the topic.

- 'Honour is the reason why we live. Without it life is pointless,' says a young girl from Şanlıurfa.
- 'Your honour is your wife,' says a man aged twenty-five, from Istanbul. In saying 'wife' he used the word *helalın*: someone to whom you have a right.
- 'As the elders say, a man's most sacred possessions are his horse, his woman and his gun. Honour is a woman's duty. If she tries to betray you, it means you've lost your dignity,' says a man aged thirty-nine from Adana.
- 'For me honour is everything… If I had a wife, she would be my honour. My sister is my honour too, and so are my female relatives – my uncle and aunt's daughter. Everything that happens around me and my family is my honour,' says a man aged twenty-four, from Batman.
- 'A woman of honour should be attached to the home and to her husband. She cannot do anything that might prompt gossip. She should not tell stories about things that happen in her home. She cannot go to her mother and say: "Mama, my husband beats me." Or "I want a divorce",' says a woman aged twenty-five, from Batman.

Yet the essential meaning of honour was rendered best by a young man from Istanbul: 'When I hear the word "honour" the only thing that comes into my mind is a woman. Nothing else.'

According to a liberal journalist from Ankara: 'For them, honour lies between a woman's legs.'

Professor Ertürk notes that the most uncompromising attitude towards punishing women is shown by uneducated men aged from sixteen to twenty.

7

It all starts with a rumour. So I am told by Kurdish director Mehmet Sait Alpaslan, who has written a film and a play about the death of Şemse Allak.

The rumour arises suddenly. It can be triggered by an ordinary look or a smile, as a man is walking along the road. But sometimes there's no need for a reason. It's enough for someone to say a single word, and then for someone else to add a second one.

At first the rumour is like a falcon: it circles high overhead. From that height it can't do any harm. Sometimes it flies off, and the danger passes.

But sometimes it comes down and gets to people, feeding on their bile, regret, poverty and envy. Evil people nourish it, until it gains the strength to enter the village.

It comes in like a hunter. The victim still doesn't know a thing, but the verdict has already been reached. Rumour leads to being cursed, which leads to the dagger. The killer has sharpened his knife.

It doesn't matter if it's true or not. Who would think of checking? What matters is that she's tarnishing the family honour.

The rumour is far more important than the truth. The truth won't set her free. All that matters is what people are saying.

It's hard for me to walk about Diyarbakır with this knowledge. I take the side streets. The children here have holes in their shoes, and their mothers spend all day long sitting on the front step, gossiping. There's nothing going on. And suddenly a green dot appears on the horizon. It's getting bigger, but it's not turning into any familiar outline. The mind searches for the right word, and finds it: *yabancı*, a foreigner.

First a crowd of children waylays me. They're saying something, shouting. They're asking for sweets and dollars, but more for a laugh than in the hope that I'll give them anything. Finally there's something happening, at last there's something to kill the boredom.

Their mothers are very young, under twenty. They're smiling. They're bored too. They'd be happy to have a chat, but in this town it is the man who must speak first.

Am I to reply to their smiles? I'd like to; I enjoy this sort of meeting. But that is exactly how rumours start.

Afterwards, somebody might say one of the women smiled at me too often, or too broadly. Or that she looked at me for five seconds too long. However absurd the accusation might sound, it could cost someone their life.

Maybe it's an exaggeration, but I think my smile could kill someone, so I lower my gaze and keep walking.

8

There was a rumour circling over Hatice's head like a hawk. At the centre of every Turkish village there is a small tea house where the men sit all day long. There Abdullah whispered to several people that Ahmet's wife was a whore.

'He's only just left, and she's already offered herself to me! I slept with her. I'm going to sleep with her again today!'

In villages where nothing happens for entire days on end, the men love this sort of story. In parts of the world where virtue is more important than life, people are especially keen to listen to stories about women who lack virtue.

Abdullah's friends smacked their lips in admiration: '*Çapkın seni, abi*! What a stud you are, brother!'

Then they told their acquaintances about it, and they told theirs.

A few weeks later, the entire village was talking about nothing else.

All this time, quite oblivious, night after night Hatice had to block the door with her own body to stop Abdullah from getting into her room.

9

Nowhere in the world does a brother love his sister as much, nowhere do the children love their parents as much, or the parents their children. That's what the Turkish Kurds proudly say of themselves. So how can it be possible for the fathers to kill their daughters, and the husbands to kill their wives?

They do it out of love.

Aytekin Sır, professor of psychiatry at the university in Diyarbakır, has done research on this subject. He has visited some fifty perpetrators of honour killings in prison. Most of them will spend the rest of their lives behind bars. He asked all of them the same questions.

According to Professor Sır: 'Honour killing is not a crime of passion, when a guy finds his wife with another man, grabs a pistol and shoots. It is a carefully considered process. First the family elders gather, because it all happens within clan structures. They say what has been going on, and take a decision. Then they appoint an executioner. The father or the husband often disagrees with the verdict, but there's no arguing with the elders, or you might be in for it yourself. There have been cases where a husband who refused to kill his wife has died along with her.'

'Who are the killers?'

'Someone from the immediate family. For most it's the first time they've ever killed. They're often in shock after what they've done.'

'What do they say?'

'That they have behaved properly, and that the penalty for

tarnishing the family honour is death. The entire community endorses them in the conviction that they've done the right thing. As men who defended honour, they even have a high-up position within the prison hierarchy. One of the standard questions we asked is this: "What would you say now to your wife/sister/daughter?" Most of them went to pieces at that moment. Up to this point they'd spoken of her as "the woman". Now they had to take a personal attitude. They'd say: "I'd tell her I love her, and that I did what I had to. And that I know she understands."'

'How do they explain what they've done?'

'I talked to a brother who had killed his sister because she had a boyfriend at high school. He was a normal guy – when he was at liberty he had dreamed of becoming a chauffeur. I asked if the penalty for a high-school romance should really be death, to which he replied: "She tarnished my honour. Honour is the most important thing for me. Honour is all I have." I think that is the main reason for these killings nowadays. In the villages, where there's no work, money or future, people have nothing but their honour. Those who've done well – who have a business, money and prospects – rarely kill.'

10

Halil knew by now that he wasn't going to get away with rape, and that a life was at stake. He tried to gain the imam's support. Some say the imam refused, others that at first he refused, but then he sent for Halil's and Şemse's brothers, and tried to reconcile them.

Meanwhile, the rumour was being fed at the homes of the villagers of Yalım. People were saying it was Şemse who had provoked Halil, and that a woman who has no husband at her age is sure to be a whore. And as she was a whore, she would have to be punished.

By now the rumour was as strong as a lion. Şemse's family met in secret and decided the woman must die. So at least say the people of Yalım nowadays.

But Halil did something that nobody was expecting.

11

Honour killings are committed almost exclusively by Muslims. How do they relate to Islam? Does the Quran demand the killing of unfaithful wives?

I seek the answer at a professional union of imams of the Diyarbakır district. The union leader Zahit Gifkuran, tall as a birch tree, explains that if someone suspects his wife of infidelity, he must head home with four trustworthy husbands. If they catch the lovers red-handed, the court will impose a lifelong punishment of house arrest.

'There's not a word in the Quran about the death penalty,' says Imam Gifkuran. He has nothing more to add, so our conversation is drawing to a close. But a little old imam sitting in the corner of the room wants to add something. His name is Süleyman Baznabaz, and he has spent almost his entire life working in a small village not far from Diyarbakır.

'Every woman knows she can come to me if she feels threatened,' he says. 'If she is in danger I try to talk to her family. Sometimes it only takes the intervention of someone clear-headed to put a stop to the crime. If the family is religious, they always do as I say.'

'What sort of thing do you have in mind, *hodja* [master]?'

'I'll give you an example. A girl has run off with a boy. "We'll kill her!" cries the father. And I ask: "Why don't you marry her to him? His family will give you a lot of money and some land. You'll save your honour, and in a few years everyone will have forgotten about it. Your son won't go to prison for murder."

And they agree. There was another incident where a boy took advantage of a girl without her consent.'

'He raped her?'

'So it is said. She was thirteen years old, the family wanted to spare her, but the whole village was already talking about it. So I said: "Marry them to each other! The boy won't go to prison, and the girl will come out of the matter honourably."'

'Marry her? To a rapist?'

'My son, this way I saved her life. And do you know what happened?'

'Well, *hodja*?'

'They fell very much in love. She came to me and said: "*Hodja*, I am so happy." She'd already forgotten the past.'

'And are there cases where mediation doesn't work?'

'Yes, there was a case like that. The girl was seduced by her uncle's son, and fell pregnant. I invited her under my roof until they could reach an agreement. She lived with me and my wife for half a year. I told the family I would allow the man to take a second wife, and that they only had to settle the matter of the dowry. The boy wanted to marry her, though he didn't have to. He was from a very rich family. His father could have paid compensation.'

'And what happened?'

'The first wife made a terrible fuss. She cut her own face and said she'd rather die. The girl's family refused to wait until the child was born. They broke into my house, kidnapped her and drowned her.'

12

Hatice's family elders gathered to talk about Abdullah's rumours. They decided that the girl must die. Whether she had let him into the room or not, the rumour had already gone too far.

Ahmet was away in the army, and nobody told him about this. Hatice's brother Metin was appointed to be her killer.

Metin arrived early one morning, while Hatice was milking the cows. He came up from behind and was going to stick a knife in her neck, but he couldn't do it. He was only seventeen; he had killed animals before, but it turned out killing a person isn't quite so easy.

Hatice turned around and saw her brother holding a knife. She didn't know why he had come to kill her, but the women in this region don't have to know the reason. They are familiar with scenes like this from childhood onwards. Hatice knew that if they had passed sentence on her, sooner or later they would kill her, so she ran away at that instant.

She raced as fast as her legs would carry her to Diyarbakır – a distance of eight kilometres. She herself has no idea how she got there. Once in the city, she went to the police.

The policeman asked what exactly had happened.

'My brother tried to kill me.'

'How do you know that?'

'He was standing over me with a knife.'

'Maybe he was just passing by and happened to need a knife?'

'No, he came specially for me.'

'What have you done to hurt him?'

'I don't know.'

'If you haven't done anything, he's not likely to kill you,' said the smiling policeman, and told her to go home.

Luckily Hatice had heard of the Kamer organisation before then. She decided to seek it out.

It wasn't easy. She had never moved about the city on her own before, nor had she ever had to look for any street or organisation. And asking someone the way could end badly. A young girl from the countryside alone in the street? That's not a typical scene.

But she managed it. At the foundation's headquarters the volunteers listened to her story, then helped her to find a women's refuge and promised to mediate.

13

Only a short time ago honour killings were regarded as a family matter in which nobody should interfere, but since then several media campaigns have swept across Turkey. Posters were put up in the smallest villages. Apart from Kamer, in Diyarbakır alone about thirty other organisations designed to help women appeared. Nowadays almost every woman knows where to turn in case of need.

The government is also trying to force families to send their daughters to school. Honour killing most often affects girls with no education. The ones who have come into contact with a school are capable of seeking help. Even the imams helped with the 'All Girls to School' campaign.

However, the families whose honour had been tarnished found other ways of purging themselves.

'We noticed that in our region the number of suicides among young girls had been growing dangerously,' says Professor Sır. 'In the world as a whole, it is far more often boys who commit suicide, but here things suddenly began to be different, so we started examining these cases. In Mardin a young woman had shot herself in the head. After a short interview we learned that she was left-handed, but the shot was fired from the right-hand side. After a longer one, it turned out her husband had killed her. In another case a woman had shot herself in the back of the head.'

'What?'

'They'd killed those girls, and then reported suicide. Or an accident. Outside the city of Van a tractor ran a girl over. "An accident," said the family. But when they did an autopsy on her it turned out the tractor had run her over at least forty times.'

Ayşe Gökkan researched all the suicides of young girls from Diyarbakır in 2006. 'I had the following case: before she was killed, a young wife had gone to the police several times, saying: "My husband wants to kill me." But they had just sent her home. A week later she was no longer alive. I looked at the documents: suicide. It's more convenient for the police to put that on the records, because they themselves were to blame. The problem is that they're from the same environment too. They may be in uniform, but they have the same thing in their heads as the husband and brother of a girl like that.'

According to Ayşe Figen Zeybek of the Kamer organisation: 'Opponents of Turkey's entry into the European Union say: "They kill girls. We mustn't let them join." But I say: "Nothing has helped as much in our work as the prospect of EU membership. It has saved the lives of dozens of girls! We must join, if we're going to have the power to fight this problem effectively!"'

14

Şemse ran off to the house of her rapist, Halil. She knew that her family would try to kill her.

Some say Halil took her in because he had no alternative. Others say that he really was in love with her. He hid her in the cellar and told her brothers he didn't know where she was. He thought up a plan which was meant to save them both. One night he led Şemse out into the fields in an attempt to bypass the village and reach the highway. There he would hitch a ride, or take a bus into Mardin. What he planned to do after that we shall never know.

Some say a dog woke up the village, others say somebody saw shadows stealing across the fields. Yet others say that Şemse's brothers had been hiding near Halil's house. There could be something in it, because suddenly, in the middle of the night, there was a large crowd of people in the fields. Not even the police had managed to find out how many of them there were. Who threw the first stone also remains a mystery. All that was ever established is that from twelve to eighteen people gathered there, that the men and the older women threw the stones, and that there were several children running about among them.

Halil tried to shield Şemse with his own body. He died first.

Once their anger had gone, the people went back to their beds.

In the morning, soldiers patrolling the area found two bodies lying in the middle of a field in a pile of stones.

15

Şemse Allak did not die in that field. When the soldiers found her body, she was still alive. She had lost her baby, and she was in a coma, but she was alive. She ended up at a hospital in Diyarbakır, but she never awoke. She was buried by members of the women's organisations. Nobody from her family showed up at the funeral.

In the village, a conspiracy of silence prevailed. As a result, the culprits were never punished. Şemse's brothers are still living in Yalım. Halil's wife only moved to Istanbul last year.

Three years after the stoning in Yalım I go there to talk to the inhabitants. The village is a suburb of Mardin, a city with a population of one million. At the entrance there is a large dove with an olive branch in its beak.

We tell people the European Union has sent us, and that we've come to ask about the lot of the Kurds. I'd rather not take any risks – they've already driven several journalists away with their fists. And the EU has positive connotations round here.

The men invite us for tea. They all have thick, raven-black moustaches. We sit in the village square and listen. In Yalım, of a total population of 120 people only twenty or perhaps thirty have jobs, some of them just in the summer, when there is work to be done in the fields. But most of them spend all year round at the tea house.

'What do you usually do?' I ask the youngest ones, who look about thirty years old.

'Well, we sit around. We have a cup of tea...'

Their knowledge of Turkish is weak, so my interpreter shifts into Kurdish. They liven up – all the villagers are Kurds. But they can't even watch television in Kurdish, because the Mardin town council blocks the satellite-dish signal.

'We can understand Turkish, but our wives can't,' they say.

'What other problems do your wives have?' I ask.

'A lack of medical care. The doctors don't speak Kurdish. Even the labels on the medicines are in Turkish only.'

'They can't make themselves understood in any official place...'

'What about violence? Does it happen?' I ask a dozen Kurdish husbands. According to the statistics, they beat their wives more than anyone else in Turkey.

There is a moment of dismay.

'What people do at home is none of our business,' says one of the older ones curtly. I muster my courage and ask if the tragic event of three years ago has changed any aspect of village life. They confer on what event I might have in mind. They guess it's about the stoning.

'No, nothing in the village changed after it,' the older man cuts things short.

The female weaving teacher who runs a workshop on the edge of the village is of the same opinion. A conversation with us is an act of immense courage on her part. Everyone has seen us entering her studio.

'The girls work at my place until they get married. After that it's not honourable for a husband for his wife to work. So they are from ten to sixteen years old. The day after Şemse's killing it occurred to me that it must be traumatic for them, and that I should talk to them about it.'

'And what happened?'

'I asked gently: "So you must be in shock?" And my girls replied: "She deserved it, the whore!"'

'Why do they think like that?'

'Because she was single. And because if he raped her, she must have provoked him. My pupils are imbued with this sort of thinking.'

'Has anything changed since Şemse's death?'

'People have become withdrawn. The whole country was talking about Yalım as a village full of murderers. It was the first stoning in Turkey for decades. The press wrote that everyone here has blood on their hands.'

16

When Ahmet came back from the army, Hatice asked the volunteers from Kamer to talk to him.

Ahmet didn't want to talk. The family had told him his wife had run off with another man. But when he found out she had been at a women's refuge the entire time, he just said: 'Let her come home.'

And she did.

Her father, mother and brother acted as if they didn't know her. They were sure she had slept with Abdullah. They never even asked her what had really happened. Her in-laws and the clan elders told Ahmet to kill his wife, but Ahmet believed Hatice, and rebelled.

And so he became a man without honour. From one day

to the next the baker stopped selling him bread, the tea-house owner stopped taking any notice of him, and people stopped responding to his greetings.

'You're there, but it's as if you don't exist,' says Ahmet today. 'Once I went into the tea house and poured myself some tea. An employee came and spilled it onto my shoes. Old women spat at the sight of me. To get any bread I had to walk to the city, eight kilometres. And my brothers decided to kill me along with my wife.'

At the same time, almost every day Abdullah would call Hatice and say she was going to be his – if not in this world, then in the next one.

17

Ahmet and Hatice decided not to wait for events to develop. The women's organisations found them a flat in Diyarbakır. They borrowed a little money, but Ahmet soon paid it back. He is very hard-working.

A few days after moving, they went to the village for their last remaining things. Hatice had borrowed a Dictaphone from someone. She waited for Abdullah to call.

He did. He described all the positions in which he would have his way with her. He said she was a whore and that any man could have her. Hatice egged him on.

'Why do you tell people you slept with me? I never let you into my room!' she said. Abdullah burst out laughing.

'So what? They'll kill you, but I'm going to live. If I want them to, they'll kill your father and mother too,' he said.

Next day Hatice made some copies of the tape. Ahmet sent one copy to his parents, and another to his wife's. A few days later they called on the mobile to apologise. They said the couple should come home, because now everything was clear. But Hatice and

Ahmet didn't want to live in their village any more. Since then, neither of them has ever spoken to their parents again.

Only Abdullah still lives there to this day.

18

A girl in a white dress stands centre stage. She gazes sadly at the audience and at the figures surrounding her. Now and then one of them comes into the centre and says his or her piece.

The girl in white is Şemse Allak. She has come back from the world beyond, and is listening to what her persecutors have to say.

'My daughter, why didn't I save you?' weeps her mother. 'Believe me, I wanted to! Our old traditions wouldn't let me. The fear that they might kill me too wouldn't let me!'

'Sister, don't think I'm a bad person,' her brother apologises. 'I killed you because I had to. Because we were too poor to pay for our honour. Even in prison they could see I have a good heart. That's why they let me go...'

Director and scriptwriter Mehmet Sait Alpaslan played the part of the killer-brother. He and his actors have toured the whole of eastern Turkey, and have often performed the play about Şemse in very small towns.

'The audience divides in two. One lot applauds when the mother shouts: "Kill her! She deserves to die!" And there are those who applaud and whistle during the stoning. But the most important thing is that the decided majority applaud when the imam says: "Let them live. Allah forbids you to kill."'

sinan's dream

I DON'T LIKE hiring tour guides.

They rarely say much more than I can read for myself in the *Lonely Planet* guidebook. You'll say something like: 'Take me to a place that's not typical,' and they'll take you round the corner to the nearest mosque and expect you to gawp in wonder at how unusual it is.

Anyone applying to be my guide has really got to surprise me before I'll be prepared to waste my time and money.

The guide in Edirne, the former capital of the Ottomans, looked like an impoverished teacher trying to top up his salary. He showed me around a pearl of Ottoman architecture: the fabulous, multi-storey chocolate box known as Selimiye Mosque. He was wearing crumpled trousers, an outmoded sweater and horn-rimmed spectacles. He looked like a bore, but he managed to surprise me instantly. Instead of saying: 'I'll tell you about the greatest mosque in Turkey,' he said: 'I'll tell you about the architect Sinan's greatest dream'.

At once I was all ears.

1

'Only one architect like Sinan is born in a thousand years. They call him the Turkish Michelangelo, but Michelangelo wasn't fit to tie his bootlaces – he had the luck to be born in the West, while Sinan was born in Turkey. To this day it is hard for a Turk to make a breakthrough abroad,' says the guide in crumpled trousers regretfully. As proof he shows me the sultan's fantastic tiled loggia. 'Sinan's father earned his living making gravestones. He was a Christian. And so as a young boy Sinan ended up in the Janissary corps, the crack troops recruited from among the sons of infidels.

'In Istanbul he soon turned out to be extraordinarily talented. He became a junior commander, then a senior one, but it even more rapidly transpired that what he did best was construction. They say he was already fiercely ambitious then. This ambition ate away at him from the inside like a worm.

'His first serious piece of work was Haseki Hürrem, a *hamam* (or bathhouse) for the wife of Süleyman the Magnificent. This wife was called Hürrem, but you foreigners call her Roxelana. She was a captive from Poland, probably the daughter of a Ukrainian priest, and she happened to be incredibly beautiful. Süleyman was head over heels in love with her.

'The bathhouse is in Istanbul, standing between Hagia Sophia and the Blue Mosque. Today they sell carpets there. The sultan liked it, so Sinan received further commissions – first a bridge, then a mosque, then the tomb of an important general.

'Throughout his long life he built mosques, madrasahs, Quranic schools, hospitals, *caravanserais*, aqueducts, palaces and baths. For Süleyman the Magnificent he built the Süleymaniye Mosque complex, which still towers over Istanbul. Everyone admired him.

'But he was never satisfied with himself, nor could he ever be, because he was being eaten away by the worm of ambition. And above his city of Istanbul there towered a great ulcer.'

2

'There is no other building in the world like Hagia Sophia – the Church of Holy Wisdom,' says my guide in the horn-rimmed specs, as he leads me into a garden where Muslims can relax after *namaz*, or prayers. 'For almost a thousand years it was the tallest temple in the world. It was only outclassed by the cathedral in Seville, which dates from the early sixteenth century, and which, please note, was built on the site of a former mosque,' he tells me. 'At its highest point the cupola is fifty-five metres high. It was built in barely five years! Both the speed and the results of the work performed by the Byzantines is impressive to this day.

'When Mehmed the Conqueror took Constantinople in 1453 and entered the city in triumph, he decided not to destroy Hagia Sophia. He simply gave orders for the basilica to be converted into a mosque. Thus at the very centre of his new capital he retained a festering ulcer.

'Though their jaws dropped at the sight of the sultan's and his country's riches, all the infidels would finish by saying: "But you have failed to surpass Hagia Sophia". And whatever the sultan did, whatever conquests he achieved, still the infidels kept saying: "You have failed to surpass Hagia Sophia".

'They were right. And we, the Turks, have never cared about anything as much as the admiration of the infidels. We ourselves are incapable of appreciating what we have and what we represent. It is only admiration in your Western eyes that can give us a sense of our own value. And so from one year to the next the ulcer continued to fester more and more.'

3

'Sinan was far more badly stung and inflamed by the ulcer in the form of Hagia Sophia than others,' says the guide who looks like a teacher topping up his pay, as he shows me a place for performing ablutions. 'He was the greatest architect the sultans had ever had. He was the one who should take up the gauntlet cast down generations ago, and build something bigger and more beautiful. The biographers say that Sinan lived to a ripe old age – and he lived almost a hundred years – purely because of Hagia Sophia. That was what gave him the strength to get up in the morning and work until late at night. It was his obsession. But none of his buildings came anywhere near the height he longed to achieve.

'The opportunity to surpass it finally came when Sinan was more than seventy years old. Selim II, son of Roxelana and Süleyman the Magnificent, commissioned him to build a mosque in the former state capital, Edirne. Apparently the sultan had dozed off while on a journey, and at roughly the height of today's Fenerbahçe football stadium the prophet Mohammed appeared to him in a dream. First he upbraided the sultan for having failed to free Cyprus from the hands of the infidels, despite having vowed to do so. By way of an apology he told him to build a mosque.

'From the start Sinan was convinced that this very mosque would eclipse Hagia Sophia. Finally he would show the infidels their place! Finally the whole world would marvel at the artistry of the Ottoman architect and praise the name of Allah!

'The old man briskly set to work, eagerly telling everyone that very soon the ulcer standing opposite the sultan's palace would cease to fester.'

4

'Barely six years later, in 1574, Selim invited the elite of Istanbul to the opening of the Selimiye,' says the guide in the outmoded sweater, leading me under the cupola admired by the cream of Istanbul society hundreds of years ago. 'Though their eagerness was great, the elite shook their heads, smiled disdainfully and whispered that the sultan and his court architect had lost their wits. The mosque did not seem to them a centimetre higher than Hagia Sophia. What's more, they thought it looked much smaller.

'Sinan heard their whispers and was offended. He alone was sure the temple he had built had outdone the work of the Western designers. A few months after it was constructed he died in peace. And do you know what?' At this point my guide lowers his voice and looks deep into my eyes. 'Sinan was right. In the 1970s some Americans came here and measured it all very carefully with a laser. It turned out that Selimiye's cupola is higher than Hagia Sophia's, by exactly two centimetres.'

5

The guide presses my hand and stuffs the money he has earned into his shirt pocket – the entire sum, though I could have haggled with him, because he did embellish Sinan's life a bit. But then we hadn't agreed on a conversation about history, but about dreams.

So I have another conversation about Selimiye Mosque with Haci Murat Özçanoğlu, an architect from Istanbul.

'Sinan may indeed have been convinced he had built the highest temple in the world. To this day many Turks believe that, but they're wrong. The cupola is about twelve metres smaller than the cupola of Hagia Sophia, but it stands higher up, so it might look as if it's close in height. It's only the diameter of the cupola that's a little bigger, exactly half a metre.'

Nor is it true that Sinan died straight after completing this building. It was the sultan who died a few months later – the architect lived another fourteen years. He went on working and wrote his memoirs. He never accepted that Hagia Sophia had defeated him.

imams and condoms

TAYFUN AND ÖZGE have been living together for a year in Istanbul. They sleep in the same bed. What's different about them?

'Absolutely no sex at all,' says Tayfun, smiling sadly.

He is a musician and poet, she is a graphic designer. They lead a rock-and-roll lifestyle: parties, guests and alcohol. They don't look like radicals, and yet Özge confirms that it's true.

'I have to be tough. He's a Kurd,' she says, glowering at her boyfriend.

how the beast in tayfun awakes

Tayfun has a hangdog look on his face. Is it his fault he was born in the conservative east?

'But darling...'

'Tayfun, I know what you're going to say! That you're different from those troglodytes. That you wash the dishes and do the hoovering.'

'No man in my family has ever done that! But I do. Because I love you. I'm not like they are!'

'All you men want just one thing!' shouts Özge, throwing a packet of cigarettes at him.

'But you want it too, don't you, *findikim**!'

'*Do* I?'

Özge takes a deep breath. Tayfun has hit the bullseye. Yes, she would like it too. She too can see it's not normal. All her friends are doing it, and they're adults, aren't they?

Sometimes they start kissing before they go to sleep. It's nice, but she can tell the beast in him is just about to awaken. What does that mean? It means he won't obey her; she'll say: 'Stop,' and he'll say: '*Findikim*, my petal, my little cloud, let's do it, just this once.' Then she'll say: 'Get your hands off!' And he'll say: 'What hands?'

'Do you watch out in case he's getting aroused? That's sick!' I say, and Tayfun joyfully claps me on the back.

'It's normal caution,' says Özge, shaking her head.

'But why can't you go any further?'

'Go and ask a Turk if he'll marry a girl who isn't a virgin.'

This time it's Özge who has hit the nail on the head. Although thinking about sex occupies a large part of his day, the average Turkish man wouldn't dream of marrying a woman who isn't a virgin. That's why girls often put off the decision to go all the way until their wedding night. According to research, for eighty per cent of them, their first sexual partner is their own husband.

But that's just a statistic. The gynaecological clinics make a fortune on discreet operations to sew up torn hymens.

'I could do that too,' says Özge. 'But despite having a population of fifteen million, Istanbul is like a big village. A colleague of mine had herself sewn up, and the next day all her friends knew about it. It turned out the receptionist at that private clinic was her ex-boyfriend's cousin.'

And so Özge has to take more radical steps. If the beast in Tayfun awakes, she gets up, puts on the light and switches on the

---

* A term of endearment meaning 'little nut'.

TV. If he gets annoyed, she goes into the other room and waits for his mood to pass, and if it doesn't, she sleeps on the sofa.

Sometimes the beast refuses to go away, and then Tayfun goes to sleep at a friend's place for a few days.

'What's the point of it all?' I ask. 'Won't Islam let you?'

'I'm not bothered about that. But he's from the east. Out there a woman without virtue is worth nothing at all. If I sleep with him, he'll cease to respect me.'

'You've been together for two years. If it were just about sex, he'd have left by now.'

'You'll never understand. You're not a Turk.'

how to burn off your hair

Özge may be right. She tells me about her female friends who have kept the same boyfriends for a year, or two, or five. In each of these stories the girl finally gives in, and in each one – right at the end – the boy leaves her. Is she exaggerating? Or maybe she has strange friends? Or maybe her friends have strange boyfriends? It's hard to tell.

In 2005 the Turkish newspaper *Hürriyet* publishes a major report on sex in Turkey, known as the Turkish Kinsey report. Here are some of its most interesting facts:

- forty per cent of men do not know what the menopause is;
- one in three women never thinks about sex at all;
- couples (before marriage) make love for an average of 8.2 minutes per month, preceded by 11 minutes of foreplay;
- half of all women cannot define or describe an orgasm.

Comedy writer Metin Üstündağ offers the following comment on the results: 'In Turkey most people think "Theclitoris" is the capital of Singapore.' But take away the religious east, and Turkey would come out twice as modern. 'It's those cave-dwellers who bring down our results!' fume the people of Istanbul. So I ask a man who represents the backward east and a clearly enlightened man from Istanbul to tell me about their sex lives.

Metin is twenty-one and he comes from Konya, in the heartland of conservatism. He is studying economics. Serdar is twenty-five and comes from a rich family. He is a student at a private university. We meet at the apartment he rents with some friends.

'When I reached the age of seventeen, my brother took me to a brothel,' says Metin. 'Now I go there every month with friends from my student hostel. We wash and shave...'

'Do you burn off your hair?' asks Serdar.

'Yes, we do.'

Turkish boys are obsessed with being too hairy. They trim or depilate their chests, and they burn off the hair in their noses and ears with a lighter. What for? Because women don't like excess body hair.

'Then what?' I inquire.

'Then we book two women and we have a good time until morning.'

'Two?'

'We can't afford more than that. They stay in a little room, and we take turns to go inside. While we wait, we smoke hookahs, drink *rakı* – an aniseed-flavoured spirit – and chat. If anyone's in there for too long, then bang! We thump on the door.'

'Do a lot of men go there?'

'Where I'm from, yes. Most of my friends are bachelors for a long time because they can't afford wives. No father will give his daughter to someone who doesn't earn much. And there are needs... Well, you know what I mean, everybody has them.'

'In Istanbul it's easier,' says Serdar. 'I had my initiation as a sixteen-year-old with the neighbours' daughter. Then after every party something always came up. The east is terribly shut off, but here there's total hedonism. I think it's Turkey's biggest sexual problem. There are very few people who sleep with each other just because they're in love.'

how to pick the neighbours' pears

According to research by the daily paper *Hürriyet*, one Turkish man in three starts his sex life with a prostitute. Only for one quarter of them is his first sexual partner his own wife.

'But,' stresses Serdar, 'consider the fact that no research on this issue is ever reliable in Turkey. The women will always say less than the truth, and the men will say more. And those who have never even kissed will tell you the most of all.'

Every second man declares that he is unfaithful to his wife or partner. But here the data add up, because as many as eighty-one per cent of Turkish divorcees give the husband's unfaithfulness as the reason for the split.

The most famous newspaper column about sex also began because of infidelity. Its author is Güzin Abla – Big Sister Güzin – also known as Fatma Güzin Sayar, a journalist from Istanbul. The biggest newspapers have been in fierce competition to publish her sexual advice for years.

In 1938, at the age of sixteen, Güzin Abla is married to a Turkish naval commander. She is head over heels in love, but it soon turns out that her husband is cheating on her left and right. Güzin Abla decides on a divorce and promises herself she'll never tie the knot with another man.

She only breaks her vow once, towards the end of the 1950s, when she marries a colleague from the newspaper office. When he turns out to be unfaithful to her too, she puts his suitcases outside the door and decides to devote the rest of her life to teaching Turkish men the art of love-making. And so a column entitled 'Güzin Abla Advises' appears in a magazine called *Son Havadis*.

Güzin Abla tries to reconcile two worlds. She explains to the conservatives that sex is not evil, and to the liberals that hedonism leads nowhere. And that the most important thing is love. She promotes virginity, fidelity and marital honesty, but she also encourages those who are already married to experiment in bed.

'Dear Güzin Abla,' writes one of her female readers in the late 1960s, 'I don't know what to do! I've found a letter from another woman in my husband's desk. He's having an affair! Help, Güzin Abla! In despair, Fatma.'

'Dear Fatma,' replies Güzin Abla. 'Men are like children. You treat him seriously, and he'll be off into someone else's garden to pick the pears. Try to shake him up. Threaten to leave. If he loves you, he'll do anything to stop you.'

The young Turkish men laugh at her old-fashioned views. 'Go to Güzin Abla,' they say, whenever somebody starts boring the company with their problems.

Nevertheless, for years on end Güzin Abla's advice is read by millions. But what always stirs her strongest emotions are letters from women who have been cheated on by their husbands. 'Turkish men are genetically programmed for infidelity,' she says in an interview, 'because it's rare for any of them to grow up from a boy into a man.'

how to cure not-good fick-fick

The reasons why a boy cannot grow up into a man are many. One of the particularly common ones in Turkey is something that sounds dreadful in English: circumcised-man syndrome. What on earth is that? The man to answer this question is

Doctor Mustafa Güneş, a sexologist. Every day of the week, a long queue of patients forms outside his consulting room.

'I am a sexologist doctor,' he introduces himself with a smile, his black moustache gleaming in the fluorescent light. He picks up a long, thin rubber balloon, which in this particular place can only remind you of one thing. In broken English (because he insists he knows the language and wants to talk in it) the doctor explains to me what this syndrome is. 'Look you!' he says, and blows into the balloon, until it becomes long and fat. 'This good equipment. This can fick-fick,' he says, rubbing the balloon against the palm of his hand. 'But sometimes man worry-worry. He has trouble. What then?'

'Then it's worse?' I try to guess.

'Much much worse!' the doctor affirms, and lets a little air out of the balloon. Now it's no longer stiff. 'But he can go on fick-fick,' the doctor advises, rubbing the balloon against his hand again. 'But it can be more worse. Sometimes a man has big worry-worry. New job. New apartment. The end with his wife. So, you have several months' worry-worry. Then what?'

'It's very bad?' I guess.

'Big worry-worry!' says the doctor gleefully, and lets some more air out of the balloon. By now it is almost empty. 'But he still can fick-fick,' explains the sexologist.

'But what does this have to do with circumcision?' I ask.

'Think a while... In our country we do not cut off this skin for infants. Here it is for big boys.' And the doctor gives me an expectant look, to see if I'll work it out for myself.

He's right. For little Turkish boys, circumcision is something like First Communion for Catholics – an initiation rite. The poor have it done in hospital, under the national health system. The rich have it done by a famous circumciser to the sound of special music. Kemal Özkan the circumciser, who is popular with Turkish politicians and celebrities, even holds special sessions, at which one hundred boys bid farewell to their foreskins forever during a *son et lumière* show. Afterwards, in little pageboy costumes, holding sceptres, they are taken to feed the ducks, to McDonald's for ice cream and to bow to old Eyüp – a warrior who fought against Byzantium and whose tomb is now the most sacred site in Istanbul.

But what does sex have to do with circumcision?

'Imagine you are seven years old. That you have penis and are not little girl you discovered only very recently. And for one year you have known they are going to do something to you. They're going to cut off a bit of it, operate you. And it will hurt. That alone is worry-worry, isn't it?'

'Yes, it is.'

'And the boys at school say they have to cut your whole thing off. And some stupid uncle confirms that it is true. Then you have huge worry-worry!' The doctor lets the last bit of air out of the balloon and energetically shakes it left and right. 'And when you are grown-up and wish to fick-fick, then the problem starts. When you think about the penis, you are afraid. And as a man you are finish.'

How is it cured? It's a lengthy job. From sexologist the doctor changes into psychologist. He takes the patients back to the origins of their fears, and asks them to talk about their penis like someone they care about, like a pal.

Doctor Güneş regrets the fact that circumcised-man syndrome is shrouded in a conspiracy of silence. As many as one in five Turkish men may have erection problems because of it, but no one ever talks about it.

'It is said like this: *sünnet* – circumcision – is super. There are no bacteria, there is greater potency. For children it is made into a big holiday: pageboy costume, sash, gold sequins. And then this pageboy grows up and cannot fick-fick. But of this nobody talks!'

'Why not?'

'In our country every man must be macho. My clients come

in secret from their wives and fiancées. Almost all in dark glasses, even in winter. A Turk would rather die than say that his equipment is not fit. He will go to the bazaar and buy Viagra. Perhaps the only thing worse than impotence is homosexuality.'

how to hold a pride march in turkey

Dear Güzin Abla, I have a big problem. I am not attracted to women at all. I thought it was just reserve, but it's more than that. Lately I have felt highly aroused when I've been with a male friend at the swimming pool. I fear the worst. What am I to do? Please help me! Metin.

Dear Metin, I feel very sorry for you. The disease you are suffering from is called homosexuality. Luckily, it can be cured. Güzin Abla.

Perhaps the only place where Güzin Abla's name does not prompt a friendly smile of approval is Lambda Istanbul, the association for gays, lesbians and sexual minorities. Üstüngel, who works for Lambda, is highly indignant at the mention of Güzin Abla.

'She's done a lot of harm,' he says. 'We've spent years working away at tolerance, and in every interview she keeps repeating: "Go and get cured, gays. Go and get cured, lesbians." Bloody hell!'

Lambda Istanbul is a very dynamic organisation. Every year, in cooperation with several others, it holds a big parade, combined with a three-day conference. Among other topics they talk about art produced by gays and lesbians and about the situation for minorities in Arab countries. Thousands of people come to the parade, more than half of whom are heterosexuals.

'The liberals are more open – it's even fashionable to have a gay pal,' says Üstüngel. 'It's worse with the conservatives.'

'For example?'

'My parents live in the countryside. For them a gay son would be a mega-disaster! So for their needs I have a fiancée, a lesbian friend who comes with me to visit my parents, and I go with her to see her mother. We've even thought of getting married, but that would be going too far. For now we're fighting for the legalisation of civil partnerships. But I don't know what I'd do if such a thing were possible...'

'Why is that?'

'All my friends in Istanbul know I'm gay. But I've always got my parents at the back of my mind.'

'What about the neighbours?'

'My boyfriend and I have had to move twice because people were starting to give us strange looks. Our society is terribly backward.'

how the actors simulated sex

In spring 1922 a respectable citizen of Istanbul called Besim Ömer Pasha made his way to the police station in the Kadıköy district to make an official complaint, namely that he had noticed that suspicious types were gathering at the Odeon cinema each night. Thanks to swift action by the police, for the first time in Turkey some degenerates were caught in the act of watching erotic films. It was an infamous affair. 'They are corrupting our children! We demand high sentences!' wrote the press.

This episode is regarded as the beginning of the sex industry in Turkey, which reached its heyday fifty years later. By 1960 the Turks had had the thrill of witnessing a lesbian couple kissing – or rather gently brushing their lips together – in a film called *İki Gemi Yanyana* ('Two Ships Side by Side').

But the premiere of the first sex film, *Parçala Behçet* ('Tear Me Apart, Behçet'), is regarded as the real start of the revolution. The premiere was a great big, stage-directed scandal. As many as seven thousand lucky viewers came to see it. The screening took place in Konya, the hub of the Islamic conservatives. Some hard-line Muslims held protests outside the cinemas and the police suppressed them. The liberals ostentatiously went to see the film several times. Meanwhile the producers went on to make dozens of sex films, and to earn millions of lira.

At the time, Turkish cinematography was on a world level. The Turks made copies of Hollywood movies, with Superman or Batman enjoying record popularity. However, as they were all made on the cheap, these days Turkey's young people only watch them for a laugh. The Turkish version of *Star Wars* – *Dünyayı Kurtaran Adam* ('The Man Who Saved the World') – deserved to be called the worst film ever made.

The sex-film boom ended in 1978. Under pressure from the gutter press, at this point the producers admitted that the actors had in fact just been pretending to have sex. Overnight the Turks stopped going to the cinema.

There was no alternative. The film-makers would just have to go the whole way. In 1979 the first fully legal Turkish porn production was made – *Öyle Bir Kadın Ki* ('Who's That Woman'). The film was shown in cinemas in both the east and the west of Turkey.

'It is a very important film,' says the sexologist, Mustafa Güneş. 'Firstly, it was a safety valve. Suppressed sexual urges provide fuel for extremists. And those were times when there was great political tension in the air; there were hundreds of terrorists and attacks.'

The film prompted an explosion of pornography in Turkey, while the political tension spawned the assassination of a journalist called Abdi İpekçi by the terrorist Ali Ağca, and in 1980 a military coup. When the military took power, the production of porn films was suspended.

'And what's your second argument in favour of it?' I ask Doctor Güneş.

'Sex education. The young boys had no one to ask what you do one-to-one with a woman. And in the film it was all shown. It did more than the volunteers do nowadays who go round the villages with bananas.'

how to put a rubber on an aubergine

What bananas? I find the answer at a mosque in Küçükköy, a tiny village at the end of the world.

It is late July. A small, shrivelled imam called Mustafa Ertürk enters the *minbar* (or pulpit). Around him – squatting and Turkish-style – sit men with long beards.

The imam starts his sermon: 'Allah rejoices at the birth of every new Muslim. He is happy when he hears the voice of a child. But when a mother has no money to give her child a spoonful of yoghurt, it is not good.'

The men swap glances. They know that – so why is the imam reminding them that in the countryside there's often nothing to put in the pot?

The imam looks at them too and strokes his beard. In his village very few of the children are well nourished. The government, which is battling with over-population in the east, has told him to encourage the men to use condoms.

'Today some kind gentlemen from the Mavi organisation based in the city of Batman are here at our village,' concludes the imam. 'They will tell you what to do to sleep with your wives and not have children.'

Aytekin, a volunteer, is waiting for the men outside the mosque. They come up, curious to know more. He gets them to sit around him, takes out a banana, and step by step he explains how to use a condom.

'I know it's primitive,' he tells me afterwards. 'But to get through to these people you have to attract their attention.

I show them a banana and I say: "This is your *patlıcan*, your aubergine". That's what they call the male member out in the countryside. "What comes shooting out of it is little Kurds. If a little Kurd enters your wife's belly you'll have a child."'

'Is that exactly what you say?'

'Man, they have no education in this sphere! If I start telling them about eggs and sperm, they'll tap their foreheads as if I'm mad. I have to speak in images. So I put the condom on the banana and I say: "You can catch the little Kurds in here." And I spur them on by saying: "But only a real man is any good at catching them!"'

'Do they do it?'

'Recently a guy who has twelve children said: "I will recommend this invention to my sons." But usually they turn up their noses. A rubber seems to them unmanly. "I am a Turk, I'm not going to put that on," I hear them say.'

how to pick up a turkish girl

Cahit is a real Istanbul *çapkın*, or Casanova. He boasts of having a new lover twice a week. He'd have more, but he has to work.

Cahit buys all his clothes from designer stores. He's wearing pointed shoes, very pale jeans and a shirt that's open down to his solar plexus. He's got a Catholic rosary round his neck – he thinks it's a great device for striking up a conversation.

We meet at a trendy café owned by Ara Güler, a famous fine art photographer.

'You get some really nice, classy chicks in here,' explains Cahit, and soon forgets all about me. 'Don't your feet hurt after a long day at work? I do a great massage...' he says to the waitress. She looks disgusted. Nevertheless, when she comes back with the beer, Cahit tries to press his phone number on her. He fails. 'Tough. Turkish girls are awful hypocrites,' he explains. 'They're bloody temperamental. They adore sex, but none of them will admit it.'

Two high-school girls sit down at the next table. Twice their age, Cahit gives them the wink, then stares hard at them. The girls leave.

'They just pretend to be inaccessible. You have to find the right key. With one you have to let her give the game away. With another you have to talk sharply, like a father. And with another calmly, like a psychologist. I've got my own formula for conversation. What is it? I go on about Islam, saying it's shitty to forbid people sex before marriage. And that sex is fabulous. We seem to be talking about religion, but the chick starts to think about sex.'

We leave the café. One last time, Cahit tries to press his phone number on the waitress. No chance.

'You probably think I'm tiresome. But here the basic rule is this: be brazen. Otherwise you'll waste the whole night and several hundred lira. Tip them the wink right away, start talking right away, talk about sex right away. Here we've got the highest number of girls in Europe with whom not even David Beckham could score. So if you don't want to remain a virgin, don't mince your words.'

A little later Cahit becomes pensive.

'But you know what, when I marry it'll be real love. I'll fall for her, and I'll spend two years waiting for her to agree to go to bed with me. I'll keep insisting, but she'll keep saying "no". I'll make threats, but even then she won't agree. I want to be her first and last.'

'Cahit, but... why?'

'You'll never understand. You're not a Turk.'

how to measure with a ruler

Güzin Abla died in 2006 at the age of eighty-four.

Her death inspired the Turkish journalists to take a close

look at Turkish morality half a century ago and now. 'Very little has changed,' concluded a journalist from one of the most widely read dailies. 'Women are mortally afraid of sex before marriage; husbands betray their wives; fathers are afraid of their sons becoming gay; and every second guy anxiously measures his penis with a ruler and buys Viagra at the bazaar. If nothing has changed, what did Güzin Abla give us? She may not have changed us as a society, but she did change hundreds of thousands of individual human lives.'

Doctor Güneş is also a big fan of Güzin Abla: 'This was a big woman! She said: it is not sex that is most important, but love.'

The trouble is, Güzin Abla was on her own.

'We need major, nationwide sex education,' says Doctor Güneş. 'We need a Güzin Abla in every Turkish school. Not to encourage fick-fick, but to explain: love before all. How can you not teach the young people about sex in a European country? We all know they're doing it anyway!'

For a while we sip our tea in silence. Then the doctor half asks and half sighs: 'Poland is a hundred years ahead of us, I suppose?'

at the foot of mount ararat

1

'EVERYBODY HATES US.' Mustafa soaks his moustache in Efez beer and lets his gaze roam across the faces surrounding us. He's on a downer; perhaps he shouldn't have had a third pint. Unfortunately that's often what happens when a Turk wants to cheat Allah and drink a little alcohol behind his back. So I nod understandingly, and join him in looking around the room.

In the corner a small group of Belgians are enjoying themselves. They've just come back from an expedition to climb Mount Ararat. It took them almost four days, so now they're taking farewell pictures of each other and having a good time, and they're as tanned as Indian scouts.

In another corner, under a map of the area, five grizzled men in baggy trousers with the crotch at knee height are drinking a bottle of aniseed-flavoured *rakı*. One of them is wearing a cute little hat with a pompom.

'Kurds,' whispers Mustafa, though it is the most obvious thing in the world. We are in the region where the Kurds, a race of twenty-five million with no country of their own, are in the majority. 'They hate us the most. Look what they've hung up in here.'

Behind the bar, as everywhere in Turkey, hangs a portrait of Atatürk. And that's fine. But hanging on the wall, the flag of the PKK – the Kurdish guerrilla movement – really jabs you in the eye. Next to it there is a portrait of PKK leader Abdullah Öcalan, who has been locked away in a Turkish jail for a good few years now.

'That's not on! I'll smash their bar to bits,' says Mustafa, flaring up – rather too loud. The Kurds under the map raise their heads and watch us expectantly. Mustafa is the only Turk in here, and the gentlemen in baggy trousers look as if they may have knives, grenades and Kalashnikovs in their pockets. If my friend gets too wound up, we're both in for a hiding. At best, we'll end up with slashed faces. At worst, we'll leave here in plastic bags. Incidents of the kind have been known to happen before now.

2

The bar is almost on the mountainside, on the outskirts of a town called Doğubeyazıt.

It really is a bad place to start a brawl. This is where the borders of Turkey, Iran, Armenia and Azerbaijan meet. Here you can run into tourists, smugglers, people traffickers, prostitutes and apparently even spies. The Kurdish guerrillas have often gathered on the slopes of Ararat to launch anti-Turkish rebellions, so the neighbouring towns are surrounded by army posts, and there are soldiers on guard at the city limits.

But here you can also run into lunatics who go digging up the area in search of Noah's Ark. Apparently after the Flood it came to rest somewhere around here. The Kurd standing behind the bar is telling a story about a Japanese man who was recently killed by a pack of wild dogs. He had army maps, a very sensitive metal detector and a Bible in Japanese with the chapter about the Flood highlighted.

'He got out of his car, took about ten paces, and they attacked him. One of them bit through an artery,' says the barman, and goes back to pouring alcohol.

3

'So Witold, do the Poles respect the Turks?' Mustafa suddenly asks, so I take advantage of the opportunity to distract him from the Kurds, their flags and their leaders.

I tell him the story of the sultan who during the partitions always used to ask if the envoy from Lechistan (the Ottoman name for Poland) had arrived yet. I tell him about Marshal Piłsudski, who treated Atatürk with respect and friendliness, and about the Polish village on the Bosporus which until quite recently was famous for having the one and only domestic pig farm in Turkey. In short, my dear Mustafa, the Poles respect the Turks as few other nations do.

Mustafa is happy. He nods in satisfaction, and says in that case we must drink to Polish-Turkish friendship.

Later on he asks me to tell him about my journey. What is there to say? I finished my degree, packed my backpack and set off with N., a female friend from the same year, to hitchhike from Warsaw to Jerusalem. We've travelled right across Turkey, Syria and Jordan. And after that, halfway across Israel. We've argued almost non-stop, and each of us would gladly have gone our own way by now, but we've come too far and have no money to get home. So now we're travelling in symbiosis: thanks to N. it's easier to hitch a ride, and thanks to me it's reasonably safe.

Mustafa asks if we can't afford a train or a plane. I explain that we can't, but that what counts most is the adventure, the adrenaline, and the people we meet on a daily basis. Such as him. He was driving his lorry, he stopped, picked us up and brought us all the way here. Now we're sitting here, having a beer, and it's nice. Where else would I have met a lorry driver? And I've found out far more about Turkey from people like him than from two terms at Istanbul's Marmara University.

Mustafa nods understandingly.

'You're right about that. You'll always learn a lot from a driver. Nobody has as much time to think as a professional driver. And you know what I thought of?'

How on earth should I know?

'That everybody hates us and spits on us. Both the East and the West. Do you know why that is?'

No, I don't.

'Because we're the best. The best of all!' says Mustafa, and wants to drink to Polish-Turkish friendship again. 'You're not bad either,' he says, nodding with approval. 'The Germans are all right. And the British. But we are the best. That's why the ayatollahs hate us.' And he waves his hand roughly towards the border with Iran. 'They're afraid of us. They're jealous. So are those liars too.' This time he shakes his fist in the direction of Armenia. 'Only the Azeris say they love us. But they hate us too. Because an Azeri is a sort of half-Turk. An inferior version.'

I try to quieten him down, but it's like trying to stop a horse that is just building up to a gallop.

'The Arabs?' says Mustafa, snorting with superiority. 'Ever since we ceased to rule them they've never stopped beating each other up. If it weren't for the oil they'd still be riding camels. The Americans? When we were a world power we managed far better than they do. The Kurds? They shake in their shoes at the very sight of a Turk. Anyway, there's no such thing as the Kurds! There's no such nation!'

The gentlemen under the map freeze with their glasses in their hands. I'm dying a death. Even the Belgians, who've just been showing each other pictures on their digital cameras taken from the peak, can tell there's something serious going on and stop talking. Luckily Mustafa stops talking too.

The younger of the Kurds stands up, looks in our direction and speaks, slowly chewing each word four times.

'Do all Turks have the same complexes as you?' he asks, glaring at us for a moment, and finally sits down.

Mustafa gazes uncertainly around the bar. He too has realised that a brawl is not the best idea. But after a while he leans towards me and says very softly, so that nobody else can hear: 'Didn't I tell you they're afraid of us?'

moustachioed republic

THE CROWD at the stadium in Istanbul has gone crazy. Now and then the doctors carry out an old dear who can't cope with the heat. It's a wonder no one has died.

It is 15th July 2007, the final weekend before parliamentary elections which have been brought forward. The city's residents have been waiting since morning to be as close as possible to the stage. They are festooned in flags representing his party, and they have pictures of him stuck to their brows, balloons with his portrait in their hands, and stickers on their backs, caps, whistles and emblems – the complete set of items you can put on to show your support for a favourite politician.

Finally he appears. Recep Tayyip Erdoğan, Prime Minister of Turkey, comes onto the stage and blithely waves to the crowd. The people throw flowers to his feet. He can barely utter two words before they interrupt him with cheers.

Above him there's an enormous banner with his face on it fluttering in the breeze. What's the most eye-catching thing about it? His neatly trimmed moustache the size of a small car.

how erdoğan scared the whole world

In Turkey you can recognise the politicians by their moustaches.

The nationalists have the longest ones. The socialists' are slightly shorter, and the shortest ones belong to the Islamists.

The nationalists' whiskers are well groomed, trimmed along the upper lip. The tips hang down their chins, creating a horseshoe shape which runs to the point where the face ends and the neck begins. In Turkish their party is called the MHP – the Nationalist Action Party. Its average voter dreams of a strong Turkey and is opposed to integration with the EU. They only go to Turkish resorts for their holidays, and curse the fact that there are so many foreigners there.

The socialists have a small feather-bed under their noses, which comes right down to their teeth. If it isn't groomed, it creeps into the mouth. The voters like them. The biggest socialist party was founded by Atatürk himself. In Turkish this party is called the CHP – the Republican People's Party. Its average voter does not go to the mosque, drinks alcohol and sometimes goes on holiday to the West, sometimes to Turkish resorts.

However, the ones who take the greatest care of their moustaches are the Islamists. Theirs are exactly the same size as the space provided for them by nature, and they keep them trimmed to a length of no more than five millimetres.

Over the past half-century, the Islamists have lost all possible elections. The Turks were afraid they would introduce sharia law – religious law based on the Quran – and that they would distance Turkey from Europe, and bring it closer to Iran. The average voter for the Justice and Development Party (AKP in Turkish) is supposed to have a five-millimetre moustache, and his wife should wear a headscarf. He should hate Europe, give alcohol a wide berth and approve of flogging for adultery.

That is the reason why the world froze in horror when the gentlemen with five-millimetre moustaches won the elections in Turkey. Their leader is Recep Tayyip Erdoğan.

how erdoğan works miracles

Prime minister Erdoğan is an expert at working miracles and achieving the impossible. He has a special diploma to prove it, signed and sealed. And plenty of evidence. Let's take the most recent example.

In 2007, two months before the elections, the streets of Turkey's biggest cities are brought to a standstill by opponents of the government. In Ankara, Izmir and Istanbul people are burning effigies of Erdoğan and saying they've had enough of the Islamist government. They shout: 'Down with sharia law!' and wave placards saying: 'Keep Turkey free of religion'.

The protestors don't want one of the five-millimetre moustache-wearers to become their president. For in April, Prime minister Erdoğan announced that the AKP's candidate for president is Minister of Foreign Affairs Abdullah Gül.

In Turkey the president is elected by parliament. As the AKP holds the majority of seats, it looked as if Gül was guaranteed success. However, the opposition did not attend the vote, and the Constitutional Tribunal acknowledged that without a quorum the election was invalid.

Then the AKP decided to change the constitution and to have the president chosen by general election. That was when the demonstrations began.

A protest involving two million people is bound to make an impression on any politician, especially if at the same time the army's general staff is sending the prime minister warning signs: if Gül doesn't withdraw, anything might happen. They have to be taken seriously. In the past century, the Turkish military have carried out as many as four *coups d'état*.

So it is declared that early parliamentary elections will be held on 22nd July.

The opposition flexes its muscles. The mass protests put wind in its sails. The moustachios seem doomed to inevitable defeat.

Nevertheless, when the elections come, it is the Islamists who carry off yet another triumph in a series of major successes. How can it be possible? It's a miracle! First of all, in less than a year Erdoğan created the party that won the elections and independently formed a government. Then this government initiated membership negotiations with the European Union, which Turkey had failed to start for half a century. It improved relations with the neighbouring countries and avoided getting caught up in the war in Iraq. That's not enough? The lot of the Kurds and of Turkish women has improved, the economy is running like a well-oiled machine, and only fans of Atatürk still refuse to believe the moustachios are well-intentioned.

how erdoğan packed a punch

A small boy hangs by his arms, his body stretched like a piece of string, howling with pain. His hands are tied to the ceiling. His father glares at him angrily. 'Now are you going to try swearing again?'

'From then on I never, ever swore again,' recalls Tayyip Recep Erdoğan. He often stresses the fact that his father's heavy hand had a major effect on him.

He spent his childhood in Kasımpaşa, an Istanbul workers' district famous for pickpockets and street gangs. His father came there from the Black Sea coast in search of a better life. They lived in poverty. Like many of his contemporaries, the little Tayyip earned extra money after school, selling *simit* – sesame rings – and lemonade.

The men of Kasımpaşa are impulsive and deathly proud, and it is easy to drive them to fury. It was there that Erdoğan learned to thump his fist against the table whenever something displeases him.

Ali Rıza Sivritepe, a childhood friend, gave the following memory of the prime minister to the Turkish press: 'He even had to be the best at kite-flying and at playing ball. His kite had to fly the highest. And if he lost, he was instantly in a bad mood.'

Sivritepe adds that Erdoğan was never in any gang.

'But he knew how to pack a punch,' says Hasan Özlam, laughing, who grew up on the same courtyard as Erdoğan. We meet over a cup of tea not far from the old mosque in Kasımpaşa. 'He never stopped to think about it – he just punched you in the gob, backhanded. Like that!' And Hasan demonstrates on himself how the future prime minister once laid into him. Two quick blows, and Hasan, despite being older, was lying on the floor. 'He always struck first,' he stresses. 'He would never stop to think for a split second. That hasn't changed!'

Kasımpaşa hasn't changed much either since little Tayyip was flying kites there. The men sit in the tea houses which are their exclusive reserve, sipping their tea and playing *tavla* – the Turks' favourite board game, also known as backgammon. Women in headscarves and baggy harem pants are doing the laundry.

'Erdoğan? We love him! He's our angel!' they say.

'He never gets above himself. Even as mayor of Istanbul he only ever had his hair cut at my place,' boasts Ali the barber.

'He bought his baklava at mine,' says the owner of a small cake shop.

'He helped his wife to carry the shopping,' says the baker's wife.

'He's the prime minister, I'm nobody,' adds Hasan Özlam. 'He could turn his back on me. But he points a finger at people like me and says: "I'm one of them. I'm old pals with Hasan!"'

'That's the secret of his success,' says Mustafa Akyol, a journalist for *Hürriyet* who specialises in Islam and its influence on politics, and who in private is a practising Muslim. 'The average Turk can look at Erdoğan and say: "He lives just as I do!

The family is what matters most to him. He loves his country, and he respects tradition. I'm going to vote for him!'"

how erdoğan surprised the saintly man

Once there were four men with moustaches.

The most religious of all was called Bülent Arınç. He also had the greatest support among the party grass roots. First he became speaker to the Turkish parliament, and later deputy prime minister. He became famous when he came to a press conference toting a large advertisement for tights featuring a pair of sexy legs, in order to show 'the sort of images that should be banned in Turkey'. Nothing ever came of the ban, but the tights got some free advertising.

Abdullah Gül was the educated type. He graduated in the West and liked to use expressions that other people didn't know. First he became prime minister, then foreign minister. After winning yet another parliamentary election, Erdoğan could finally make him president.

Cem Tenekeciler was the most mysterious from the start. He soon withdrew from party life, and nowadays no one knows what he's up to.

Recep Tayyip Erdoğan wasn't the cleverest, or the most religious, but he had extremely good organisational skills, and charisma, which the others lacked.

In 2001 all four of them founded the AKP – the Justice and Development Party, the symbol of which is a shining yellow light bulb. It was meant to distinguish them from the hopeless, corrupt and compromised parties of the establishment.

However, there would never have been any moustachios nor any Islamist government if not for a saintly man from the Black Sea coast called Necmettin Erbakan. The moustachios met within his party, Refah (the Welfare Party). Erbakan was a superb engineer and inventor. 'I had a career in that field ahead of me, but Allah told me to get involved in politics,' he once explained in an interview.

His collaborators called him *hodja* – the holy man, the master. They dreamed that thanks to him Turkey would return to its Islamic roots, and that after eighty years of religion being shunted onto the sidelines, the nightmare would finally be at an end.

In the 1990s the Welfare Party gains popularity mainly thanks to the poor, to whom it distributes food parcels and coal, and provides help looking for work.

In those days Erdoğan too regards the *hodja* as a saint. He works for the Istanbul public transport company, and is a diehard Muslim. He will not offer his hand to women, he fulminates against shops selling alcohol, and disdainfully calls the European Union a 'Christians' club'. He repeats after his master that 'we shall alight from the tram named democracy at the first stop we can'. But he is not considering a major career in politics.

Until the day his boss drags him over the coals and tells him to shave off his five-millimetre Islamic moustache.

'In a secular state it is not appropriate for a public servant to have something like that on his face,' he says.

'I'd rather die,' replies Erdoğan, and resigns from his job.

This humiliation is a real watershed in his life. From this moment on he builds an extremely rapid political career. The *hodja* regards him as his most talented pupil, and Erdoğan repays him by winning the election for the mayor of Istanbul, Turkey's richest city. To gain victory, he runs his campaign at discotheques and brothels. For the requirements of politics he even learns to offer his hand to women, although Islam forbids it, and afterwards the future prime minister prays for forgiveness.

When he wins, the *hodja* weeps with joy.

But the new mayor and the other moustachios are finding Erbakan's programme less and less appealing. They reckon it's time to change course. They call the group of flatterers gathered around the *hodja* the Politburo, and they call themselves the reformers. Erdoğan is the only one in the party who ostentatiously stops kissing Erbakan's hand in greeting (kissing the hand and putting it to your brow is a sign of respect for your elders in Turkey).

In 1996 Necmettin Erbakan becomes prime minister within a coalition government. In a matter of months he brings relations with the West to a complete standstill and goes on an enthusiastic tour of the Arab countries. He promises to create an Islamic union, from Morocco to Kazakhstan, and vows to liberate Jerusalem. He humbly listens to Gaddafi, who publicly rebukes him for the fact that Turkey is not Islamic enough. Yet the *hodja* gets ahead of himself during a visit to Egypt, when he promises to introduce sharia law in Turkey. From now on, the Turks are counting the days until his cabinet collapses.

In 1997 the army takes Turkey's affairs into its own hands for the fourth time in the country's post-war history. The fourth coup is the fastest yet. Tanks roll down the streets of Ankara, and one of the generals calls prime minister Erbakan to suggest that he should resign. Without a murmur, Erbakan hands over power. The majority of Turks are not even aware that anything is up.

This *coup d'état* is a key moment in Erdoğan's life. A friend of his tells me about those days as follows: 'He hates to lose. And he realised the fight for sharia law and an Islamic state would doom him to defeat. He realised he had to make concessions. That was the start of his great transformation.'

Following the army's intervention, the *hodja* is banned from being active in politics for five years and the Welfare Party is delegalised.

The people from the Politburo immediately found the Virtue Party,* but the court delegalises that too. A few months later, when the *hodja* sets up the Happiness Party, Erdoğan is no longer at his side. He has left, along with the other moustachios, to found the Justice and Development Party – the AKP.

'Traitors,' says Erbakan. 'They don't mean a thing. We shall sweep them away at the elections.'

A year later the AKP wins the parliamentary elections and forms the government independently. The *hodja* does not pass the ten-per-cent electoral threshold.

how erdoğan went to prison

The clang of prison doors closing shut – Erdoğan won't forget that sound for a long time. 'It was in 1999. A turning point in my life,' he will later tell a *New York Times* journalist. 'A man grows up very fast in prison.'

How did he end up there? At a rally in Siirt, his wife's home town, Erdoğan paraphrases a poem by an Ottoman poet. 'The mosques are our barracks, their domes are our helmets, their minarets are our bayonets, and the faithful are our soldiers,' he said. For these words he is brought before the court, which sentences him to ten months in prison for inciting religious war. He serves four.

According to a political analyst who heads one of the Turkish think tanks: 'Where there are soldiers, there's war. If there's war, against whom? Against the Turkish government!

---

* Founding new political parties is everyday fare for the Islamists and Kurds. The Turkish courts frequently delegalise their parties, so the Islamists and Kurds often found new ones. If the court delegalises the party regarded at the time as the leading one, its members quickly transfer to another.

Erdoğan told his people they were at war with Turkey. That was how he thought at the time, there's no denying it.'

This is how Erdoğan excuses himself in the press for his unfortunate recitation: 'That poem was in the school textbooks, as approved by the Minister of Education. I just changed a few words. I wanted to focus people's attention and infuse them with spirituality.'

According to Professor Metin Kaya of the University of Marmara: 'Nonsense. At that point he was still saying what he really thinks. He hates the republic, democracy and freedom. It's a good thing they locked him up. Pity it was for such a short time.'

Businessman Cuneyd Zapsu, who is a good friend of Erdoğan, interprets that prison sentence like this: 'He was jailed because the ruling parties and the military were aware of his strength. It wasn't about religion, but about preventing people from outside the establishment from gaining too much influence.'

In 1999 thousands of supporters escort Erdoğan to prison. Thousands are waiting for him on his release.

According to the journalist Mustafa Akyol: 'He came out a changed man. I thought it was the end of him as a politician, but it was only the beginning. In prison he realised that by calling for war he would never achieve anything in politics. In prison he became a democrat.'

'Nonsense,' says Professor Kaya. 'If he pretends to be a democrat nowadays, it's purely to avoid ending up in prison again. It's all *takkiye*, the old Islamic school of deceit and trickery. For the good of his family and his religion, a Muslim can lie as much he likes. Apparently even the Quran lets him do that. Erdoğan tells lies in order to introduce sharia law in Turkey.'

how erdoğan is making turkey european

In 2002 when the AKP wins the elections for the first time, Professor Kaya is horrified. Erdoğan's idiosyncratic moustache appears on the front pages of the news services worldwide. 'Is this the end of Turkish democracy?' ask the journalists.

Erdoğan patiently explains to everyone that it is not.

'I have changed,' he says. 'I know how to keep my private life separate from my public one. As a private individual I am of course a Muslim, but my party is a secular party with a liberal programme. A Turkish version of Christian democracy.'

In tune with this logic, as prime minister, Erdoğan now offers his hand to women without feeling that he's sinning. But privately he will never offer his hand to any woman, except for his wife.

As he has spent time in prison, Erdoğan cannot head the government, and so the educated type, Abdullah Gül, becomes prime minister. But Erdoğan is the power behind the throne. Although formally he does not have a function, not long after the elections George Bush invites him to the White House.

'We both believe in providence, so we're going to be excellent partners,' says Bush.

He is very much mistaken.

A few months later, thanks to the votes of the opposition and some members representing the ruling party, the Turkish parliament does not allow the USA to use its bases for an attack on Iraq. It is the first time Turkey has said no to the Americans for several decades. They are shocked.

Soon after, the AKP changes the law, and now Erdoğan can head the government. Almost from the very start he surprises everyone by initiating the most pro-European policy the country has ever had. He invites a series of EU politicians to Ankara, and fights like a lion to join the Union. According to the political analyst: 'Personally I don't understand how he can possibly have taken to it so keenly. This sort of paradox could only happen in Turkey – a diehard Muslim pushing his country towards the "Christian club".'

According to journalist Fehmi Koru, a close friend of Erdoğan: 'He has seen that the Muslims have far more freedom in Europe than in Turkey, and so he wants to transfer those rights to us.'

As chief negotiator, Erdoğan appoints a former carpet salesman.

'My family has been haggling with the Germans, French and British for three hundred years. Believe me, I know how to do it!' boasts the newly appointed chief.

According to political expert Murat Erdemli: 'Erdoğan regards negotiating with the EU as a business transaction.'

And he starts to make reforms. He allows the Kurds to use their own language and to open schools (until recently talking in Kurdish, even at the bazaar, carried a prison sentence).

On the matter of Cyprus, which has been occupied by the Turkish army for the past thirty years, he approves the so-called Annan Plan – in defiance of the island's pro-Turkish authorities. According to this plan, a united Cyprus can join the EU. However, he fails to resolve the conflict because of objection from the Greek Cypriots.

He convokes the first public conference on the early-twentieth-century massacre of the Armenians, at which historians who call these events genocide are able to take the floor. However, at roughly the same time Orhan Pamuk is brought before an Istanbul court for referring in an interview to 'the slaughter of thousands of Armenians'.

'This shows the difference between the Islamists and the Kemalists,' says one Turkish journalist anonymously. 'The latter keep Atatürk pickled in a jar and try to get all political movements to agree with him. It's like sort of a séance: making the words of the Father of the Turks fit the era of the internet and the mobile phone. If Atatürk never mentioned the massacre of the Armenians, then there was no massacre. That's why Pamuk ended up in court. And what about Erdoğan? He can see that this issue has been doing Turkey harm for the past eighty years, so he tries to do something about it.'

In 2009 Erdoğan sends President Gül to Yerevan to attend a Turkey-Armenia football match. In August of that year both countries sign an agreement about establishing diplomatic relations. And although from that time onwards the stagnation has continued on the line from Ankara to Yerevan, Erdoğan succeeds in improving relations with all the neighbours. He briefly becomes the only politician who can talk to the presidents of Syria and Iran on the one hand, and the presidents of the United States and Israel on the other. (Relations with Israel cool, however, when in May 2010 nine Turks are killed at the hands of Israeli commandos on board a ship carrying humanitarian aid to the Gaza Strip).

Yet despite Erdoğan's reforms, many EU countries openly say that they will never agree to Turkey joining the community. In response Erdoğan threatens that a rejected Turkey might team up with Russia, or with its Islamic neighbours. While he's about it, he tries to prove something to Europe which to the Turks is entirely obvious: that Turkey is part of Europe.

'In the nineteenth century, when we had major problems, they called us "the sick man of Europe". No one spoke of "the sick man of Asia!"' he reminds them at an international conference.

'Professor Huntington was wrong to talk of a battle between civilisations. Turkey is living proof that Islam and democracy can be reconciled. You just have to help us!' he tries to persuade them on another occasion.

His ministers add that having Turkey in the EU would mean security for the whole of Europe, and that in economic terms too it is not as far away as it might seem. It may be a long way from Germany, but not from newly accepted Bulgaria.

But Professor Kaya of the University of Marmara knows his stuff: 'That's *takkiye* too, it's eyewash. Why are you smiling? Before Erdoğan became prime minister, support for our entry into the EU totalled eighty per cent. Now it is around forty. Do you know why?'

'Why?'

'Erdoğan knows the Union doesn't want us. The more pressure he puts on Brussels, the more clearly Brussels makes that understood. But the Turks are proud. "You don't want us? All right then, we'll turn our backs and stop banging at your door." But if we turn our backs on Europe, towards whom will we be facing?'

'Towards Iran...'

'Exactly. And then both we, and Europe, will have a major problem. All those negotiations with the Union will lead straight to sharia law.'

'The secularists are completely lost by now,' comments Mustafa Akyol of *Hürriyet*. 'These days if you support Turkey's entry into the EU it means you're an Islamist. Today the group most strongly in support of Turkey's entry into the EU is not our elite, but women in headscarves and guys with moustaches.'

how atatürk affects erdoğan

Prime minister Erdoğan's main enemies are the Kemalists. They keep watch over Atatürk's legacy, and fight against anything that's at odds with it.

First of all, they refused to accept the existence of Islamic parties. Now, when the AKP does not refer to Islam in its programme, the Kemalists are bothered by the fact that the prime minister's wife wears a headscarf.

'The ideology of the Kemalists has not changed for eighty years,' says Mustafa Akyol. 'The world changes, and Islam changes, but the Kemalists are at a standstill.'

'That's not true!' says Professor Kaya. 'The threat that Turkey will become a second Iran is still very real. That's why the army guards our system.'

Mustafa Akyol again: 'In Turkey military rule is called democracy. Secularism in the extreme version is far more dangerous than the Turkish Islamists.'

'Why?'

'Because in Turkey, if you're religious, you can't ever have a successful career. It's just not possible! Erdoğan did a great deal of work on himself. He understood democracy and accepted it. But to that the Kemalists say: "But he's got a Muslim moustache!"'

'Do you believe in this change?'

'It's very Turkish. It perfectly illustrates how torn we are between religion and a modern state.'

how erdoğan fights for the headscarf

It is 1978. Erdoğan gives a speech at a Muslim youth meeting. At the time he is head of the Islamic youth party, National Salvation.

During his speech he notices a pair of eyes fixed on him. He seeks them out in the break. They belong to twenty-three-year-old Emine, a girl of Arab descent. They have a conversation, but she can barely form a coherent sentence. She thinks the young fellow with the moustache is the man of her dreams.

Her dreams come true, and only six months later Emine and Tayyip are engaged. From that moment to the present day Emine Hanım ('Madame Emine') is the neck that turns the head.

'She doesn't take part in public life, but she's brilliant at managing her husband,' says one of the Turkish journalists. 'She doesn't confine herself to the kitchen. Anyway, apparently she's not a very good cook. But she is quite capable of tearing a strip off Tayyip if he does something contrary to her ideas.'

In one of her rarely granted interviews, Emine Erdoğan said that the Turks should be ashamed. Why? Because they have so few women representing them in parliament. The fact that the AKP puts up more female candidates for parliament than any other Turkish party is largely to her credit.

Nevertheless, the Turks regard her as backward – because she wears a headscarf, as do the wives of all the other moustachios too. Erdoğan sent his daughters to college in the United States.

'They can go about in headscarves there,' he explained.

The headscarf is one of the fronts on which Erdoğan wages war with the Kemalists. In Turkey headscarves are forbidden at all schools and colleges. Erdoğan upholds that this is contrary to democracy, and that it deprives girls from poor families of the opportunity to study, because they are usually religious.

'The doorman asked my friend, who was studying in Istanbul, if she had come to do the cleaning,' says Mustafa Akyol. 'A woman in a headscarf might be a servant, or the janitor's wife. But a student? That's unthinkable. Even in adverts for washing powder the woman in a headscarf is always the idiot who lets the limescale build up in her washing machine, or uses "ordinary powder". It's the modern woman with no headscarf who explains to her that she has to use Calgon or Omo.'

Another front in the war between Erdoğan and the Kemalists involves religious schools, *imam hatip*. They have the normal programme for high schools, but with expanded study of Islam.

'Access to higher education is made extremely difficult for their graduates. It's unfair,' says Erdoğan. The Kemalists reply that these schools deny the theory of evolution and promote the superiority of men over women, and that the AKP is trying to train cadres of young Islamists for itself.

Yet the hardest piece of evidence against Erdoğan was his attempt to change the penal code. Erdoğan tried to introduce a penalty for adultery – either a prison sentence or a fine. He only withdrew under pressure from Brussels.

how erdoğan's friend is changing his views

To understand Erdoğan's war against the Kemalists better, I meet with Fehmi Koru, a journalist for *Yeni Şafak*, a newspaper known for sympathising with Islam. Koru, a small, stout gentleman, is one of the most important people in Turkey today – more important than the entire newspaper for which he works. Why? Because prime minister Erdoğan sets great store by his opinion. They have been friends for years, and Koru has a major influence on Erdoğan.

'If you have a chat with Koru you'll not only understand what Erdoğan is saying today, but you'll also find out what he's going to say in a year from now, in two, or even five years,' say the Turkish journalists, laughing.

Koru doesn't like to waste time, so I ask straight out: 'Does prime minister Erdoğan have some hidden purpose? Does he want to introduce sharia law?'

Koru smiles and says: 'With his capabilities, if he'd wanted to, he'd have done it by now. Indeed, he used to be an Islamist. But he has changed. I change too, so do you. Only a fool never changes his views. He was once very radical. Life has taught him that you can't be like that.'

'Why don't the Turks believe in this change?'

'Most of them do. That's why the AKP has so much support, about forty per cent. And those who say they don't believe in it are actually playing a political game. Threatening the Turks with Islamists is not justified these days. The AKP is a normal democratic party.'

'In that case why is it so concerned about introducing headscarves at universities?'

'Because the ban on them bears no relation to democracy. People should have the freedom to profess any religion.'

'What about penalties for marital infidelity?'

'That's part of the political game. Erdoğan's toughest electorate are the Muslims, the conservatives. From time to time he has to do something in tune with their way of thinking.'

In this way Erdoğan manages to reconcile fire and water. Throughout Europe he is regarded as an able reformer and a great supporter of Turkey's entry into the EU. And the Islamic countries more and more often see him as their spokesman and mediator in the West. Turkey was even going to negotiate the principles on which Syria and Israel could establish diplomatic relations. However, before this process began, the traditionally good relationship between Ankara and Tel Aviv went sour, because of the above-mentioned convoy carrying aid for the Gaza Strip and the nine Turks who were shot by Israeli commandos.

'By allowing that convoy to sail, Erdoğan was playing the role of leader of the Muslim states,' says Professor Kaya. 'But we should be sticking with the West!'

'He was standing up for the people of Gaza because their fate really is of great concern to him,' says Mustafa Akyol. 'In no way does that have to mean breaking with the West. When President Obama visited Turkey, he said we are the model for how an Islamic country should be establishing relations with Christian ones.'

how erdoğan has great luck

Erdoğan is said to be a child of fortune.

According to the political analyst: 'He must have a direct line to Allah. Maybe it's because of that diploma for performing miracles?'

'What diploma?'

'Erdoğan went to an *imam hatip* high school. Their diplomas are known in Turkey as qualifications for performing miracles. Supposedly they only teach prayers and theology, and after a school like that you're only going to find work by a miracle, but it's not true – most of those schools have quite a high standard. But Erdoğan really does give the impression of a man who knows how to chat with the man upstairs.'

'Can you give me an example?'

'Before he became mayor of Istanbul, for a year and a half we had a severe drought here. People were dying, trees were withering. When Erdoğan became mayor of the city, the clouds began to gather. The next day there was a tremendous downpour.'

'But you can't blame it all on Allah,' says Akyol. 'Erdoğan has established the best organised party in Turkey. The AKP has an office on almost every street. People can drop in there for a coffee or a glass of water, and have a chat about their problems.'

how erdoğan takes off his jacket

The AKP's election rally in Istanbul was the most important one in its entire campaign. Tens of thousands of people gathered at the stadium in the Zeytinburnu district. The location was not chosen by accident: from there you can see the stone walls which were forced by Mehmed the Conqueror six centuries ago, before he captured Constantinople and triumphantly entered it in 1453. Now these same walls were being forced by prime minister Erdoğan, in his efforts to win the election in Istanbul again.

Any Western leader would have been proud of that rally. The party showed a very modern face: among the women who appeared on stage, only the wives of the party leaders were wearing headscarves. The dozen or so female AKP candidates for parliament had their heads entirely uncovered.

Erdoğan and Gül took the floor in light-blue shirts, with no jackets, looking relaxed. They spoke calmly, only occasionally raising their voices, often repeating the words democracy, prosperity and development.

Not once during the four-hour rally did anyone say the word 'Islam'. Not once did anyone mention the word 'Quran' or the words 'sharia law'.

But the audience consisted predominantly of men with moustaches. Their neatly trimmed whiskers were rarely more than five millimetres long.

madame atatürk

1

HE'S THERE with us at the restaurant. He's there at every office as we take care of our business. He's always glowering at us from our wallets, from his portrait, and from the front pages of the newspapers. He freezes in the cold with us as we queue for the cinema, and he sweats with us at the baths. Even the lavatory attendant has a picture of him in her little cubicle.

'If ever you realise you haven't seen a single Atatürk for a whole fifteen minutes, run for it!' says Bastian, who teaches German in Istanbul. 'It means you're not in Turkey any more. You must have crossed the border without noticing.'

He's right.

From their first year at junior school the little Turks write poems and put on performances in his honour. When they grow up, they put every foreigner through a simple test. 'What do you think of Atatürk?' they ask.

If you fail the test, you can lose all your friends and acquaintances at a single stroke. And the only way to pass it is by answering: 'I think he was an outstanding statesman. Turkey is extremely fortunate to have had someone like that in charge.'

Any other answer will put you out of the game. Atatürk

has become a divinity – a monotheistic one too. Many Turks genuinely believe that he is looking down on them from heaven and helping the country. What's more, they go to the town of Ardahan in north-eastern Turkey and hold a peculiar sort of Atatürk ritual, which involves gazing at a mountain which casts a shadow that looks like the great leader's profile. The moment they catch sight of it, they dance, laugh and cry by turns, and then they have a feast.

Curiously, the very same Turks regard Islam as ignorance and superstition.

2

When Latife Uşşaki dies in her little house not far from Istanbul's Taksim Square, the newspapers hardly pay her any attention. It is 1975, and nobody but her closest circle of friends remembers her.

They bury her near the small Teşvikiye Mosque. It is not a state funeral, but the mourners drape the red-and-white Turkish flag over the coffin. Her death puts the ultimate seal on the silence of the most remarkable woman in the country's modern history.

Her story begins in the early twentieth century. As a young girl, Latife is completely different from what passes as the norm. Her father, Muammer Bey, is a cotton magnate, one of the richest inhabitants of Izmir. He has the first car in the city, and educates his children in the West. By the age of only twenty-something Latife has degrees from Paris and London, and is fluent in five languages.

After the First World War, when the powers divide Turkey like a kebab skewered on a spit, the Greeks occupy Izmir. Muammer Bey and his family escape to Switzerland. However, Latife returns to take care of her gravely ill grandmother. From all the citizens of Izmir she keeps hearing the name of one single man: Mustafa Kemal.

Soon after, troops commanded by the future Atatürk recapture the city from the Greeks. Latife does something that no other woman would have taken the liberty to do. Without any qualms she goes to see him, and suggests he should come and live at her family home.

Atatürk doesn't hesitate for an instant. Latife makes a huge impression on him; this is just the sort of woman – self-confident, independent and educated – that he will need by his side when he sets about reforming Turkey.

Four months later Latife becomes Madame Atatürk.

3

Only a few years ago Latife was a spectral figure in Turkey. The historians wrote that she was a capricious and unbearable woman who used to throw her shoes at people, insulted her friends and behaved hysterically. On top of that, she was supposed to have been as ugly as a stormy night on the Bosporus. And remarkably hairy.

How could Atatürk have taken such a dreadful woman as his wife? His hagiographers are unable to explain it. Yet it is a fact that the actual ceremony was very modern. Until that point a woman's father answered for her in all legal matters, and if he was missing, her brother or a male cousin took his place. Latife was the first Turkish woman in history to sign all the documents herself. This was a harbinger of things to come.

The marriage lasted for two-and-a-half years. Atatürk never married again, nor did he have any children.

4

In 2005 Turkish journalist İpek Çalışlar published a book entitled *Latife Hanım* ('Madame Latife'). The young wife of the 'Father of the Turks' stares at us from the cover with a bold expression. She is sitting on a horse, in a pose that says she has the whole world at her feet.

It took Çalışlar years on end to open just a small crack in the heavy door that had closed behind Latife when she stopped being Atatürk's wife. It wasn't easy. Interviewed about the book, Çalışlar complains that she failed to achieve even half of her aims. Most people refused to grant her an interview, while the letters and diary of the Mother of the Turks are lying in a bank safety deposit box, where neither journalists nor historians can make use of them.

Nevertheless, the book had an extremely wide resonance in Turkey.

'I myself was surprised,' laughs Çalışlar, when I arrange to meet her at one of the cafés on the Bosporus. 'It sold more than 100,000 copies. Thanks to my book, eighty years on, it came to light that Madame Latife had had an overwhelming influence on the fate of Turkish women. It is her we can thank for the fact that in the 1930s women could already vote and stand for parliament. It was she who persuaded her great husband to go the whole way and give us those rights.'

'Apparently she was the hysterical type?'

'Latife wanted to have a normal, loving family. But Atatürk used to spend all evening drinking and playing cards with his pals from the army. During the day he taught Turkey how to live in a modern way, but in the evenings he behaved like the typical Turkish master of the house. It upset her, and she wasn't a person who kept her emotions to herself. I'm sure she quite often screamed with rage. But hysteria? There's no evidence to say she was hysterical.'

5

İpek Çalışlar paid the same price for her book as almost any Turkish author pays for writing about a taboo subject. She was accused of insulting Atatürk, and was brought before a court.

The accuser was a reader who didn't like an anecdote the journalist had cited.

'I described how Atatürk escaped from some Greek soldiers by dressing up in women's clothing, which he borrowed from Latife. Why should anyone find that offensive?' says Çalışlar.

In Turkey, insulting Atatürk is a serious crime. This was the experience of two young girls in headscarves, Nuray Bezirgan and Kevser Çakır. They admitted on television in front of the whole country that they don't love Atatürk.

'Can I actually not love him?' Bezirgan wanted to make sure first of all. 'If I can, then no, I don't love him,' she said.

The journalist asked how she could not love the man who drove the British out of Turkey.

'If the British were here I'd have more rights than I have now,' retorted Bezirgan. 'Personally I feel closer to Ayatollah Khomeini than to Atatürk,' she added, and unleashed a storm. A day later all the major newspapers were writing about her on their front pages, and the prosecutor automatically initiated proceedings against her for insulting the Father of the Turks. The case was widely discussed in the media. It ended with an acquittal, as did İpek Çalışlar's case. The Turkish analysts regard these acquittals as proof that great changes are taking place in the country these days.

6

Madame Latife loved Atatürk very much.

'Too much perhaps,' says İpek Çalışlar pensively. 'Three times she warned him that she wanted to leave. But it looks to me more like an attempt to get him to notice that a problem had arisen in the marriage. From her friends' accounts I know she suffered greatly when it finally came to a divorce.'

Although Atatürk and Latife got married in an extremely modern way, the divorce happened traditionally. Instead of a divorce letter, Latife received a stamped government decree.

Atatürk and the former Madame Atatürk only met once again after the divorce. She was at a picnic with friends. He was sailing a yacht on the Bosporus.

'They didn't say a word to each other,' says İpek Çalışlar, 'but Latife was deeply affected by this meeting.'

For the entire remainder of her life she lived alone, only meeting with a narrow circle of her closest friends. She never talked to anyone about Atatürk, but to the end of her days she took roundabout routes just to walk past his statue.

the black girl

THE CAMPAIGN OFFICE is in Taksim, Istanbul's main leisure and entertainment district.

Inside, there's boredom in the air. The journalists have rushed off to report on the latest sensation. All that's left of them are their articles papering the walls: 'I slept with seventy-six men in a single day', 'I've had four abortions', 'For half my life I was a prostitute', say the headlines.

'It's still not enough for them,' complains Saliha Ermez, a former prostitute who is standing as a candidate for the Turkish parliament.

'They hear: "I've had four abortions", but in their eyes they've got: "Why only four? Why not eight?"' adds Ayşe Tükrükçü.

The former prostitutes run a refuge for persecuted women in Konya. The wise man Rumi, also known as Mevlana, the Saint Francis of the Islamic world, is buried in Konya. It was he who founded the order of the dervishes, who through an ecstatic, whirling dance became one with Allah and transmitted his blessing to others. Although Rumi promoted tolerance and peace throughout his life, the people of Konya are regarded as extremely conservative; former prostitutes are right off their radar.

So in 2007 Ayşe and Saliha stood in the elections for the Meclis – the Turkish parliament. By doing so, they were hoping to tell the whole of Turkey about their problems.

'Everybody wants to help children from orphanages,' they complain. 'But ex-prostitutes? People say: "That was your choice. You've only yourselves to blame!" Nobody wants to know what it was really like!'

So what was it really like?

saliha ermez's story

Saliha has dark eyes and is wearing a sky-blue T-shirt and a Muslim headscarf. As she tells me about her life, she does a lot of crying. However, she stresses, she has known for a long time how to cry and talk at once.

Marriage

I was born in a small village outside Adana, not far from the Mediterranean Sea. I had five siblings. When I was eleven, my mum fell ill. First she stopped eating. Whenever she ate anything, she immediately brought it up again. She started getting weaker, and she stopped recognising us.

When she died, the entire household landed on my shoulders. I had to clean, cook and look after my siblings. I did it as best I could, but Dad wasn't satisfied. He sent me to live with his sister. My aunt was jealous, because my uncle kept trying to touch me, so they sent me back. My father was furious.

That was when Mohammed appeared. We had met at the hospital – when my mother lay dying, his was sick as well. I didn't particularly like him, but I thought anything was better than life with my family.

My father agreed immediately. I got married at the age of just under fourteen. Where I come from, that's nothing special.

Divorce

The night after the wedding we slept together and everything was all right. But next morning the problems began.

I got up at seven. The whole family was up and waiting. My husband's mother started to push me and hit me. 'How can you sleep so long?' she shouted. 'You've got to take care of the house!'

I tried to explain that my mum had died when I was little, and that I didn't know how to keep house, but I'd learn, if they'd only give me a little time. My husband didn't say a thing. For a Turkish man, his mother is sacred.

We were together for seven years. I bore him two daughters. All that time my mother-in-law treated me very badly, and my husband always took her side. With time, they both began to beat me at once.

When I reached the age of twenty, I filed a petition for divorce. I got it without any problem. Except that in this region of Turkey a divorcee is treated worse than a prostitute.

Tea house

I went back to my family village. My brother had emigrated to Greece. My sister had got married, also as a fourteen-year-old. My father had a new wife. He believed I should go back to my husband, and that I had brought shame on him.

At the centre of every Turkish village there's a tea house. The men sit there all day long, gossiping, playing cards and making deals. To get to the local shop, I had to walk past this place, and I would hear them saying: 'I wonder who that whore slept with today'. Or: 'Ibrahim, go and ask her, she's sure to let you'. They used to laugh out loud, endlessly talking about who could have me, and who probably already had.

I had to get out of there.

Shop

I got away to Adana. I thought in the big city nobody would know me. I found a job in a shop, at first illegally. I worked on the till. I did well, so my boss wanted me to sign a contract. That was when he found out from my documents that I was a divorcee. Why do they put things like that in your documents? I don't know.

The boss transferred me to the storeroom – officially so that I wouldn't demoralise the customers, but in fact it was about something else.

The work was much tougher. I had to carry boxes, and the boss took advantage of every opportunity to grab me by the buttocks. 'You're young and pretty,' he'd say. 'You can still be used.' He wasn't bothered by the fact that he had a wife and two children. He also thought that as I was divorced, anybody could have me.

I used to spend all night crying. A few weeks later, when some people I knew introduced me to Hasan, I thought Allah Himself had come to my aid.

Hasan

He had smart clothes. He said he loved me and that I was beautiful. Now I can see those weren't great compliments, but right then it was the first time in my life anyone had ever said nice things to me.

When I told him the boss was trying to get at me, he went and gave him an earful. He said I wouldn't have to go to work anymore, and that he'd take care of me. He made me laugh, all day long, out of sheer happiness.

Friends

I went to live with Hasan. At last I felt like the mistress of the house. I didn't go to work because I was Hasan's woman. It is beneath the dignity of a Turkish man for his wife to go out to work.

Every day friends came to see Hasan. 'How wonderful,' I said to myself, 'that we have so many friends.' They drank a lot of alcohol. I know because I served them at table. 'Let them drink,' I told myself. 'It's not in keeping with our religion, but they're not causing a row or hitting each other.'

Hasan and his friends smoked strange cigarettes. I didn't know what it was. Hasan told me to light up. Obedience within the family is very important, so I lit up; nothing bad happened, so I started to smoke more often. Somehow I felt better after those cigarettes.

Hasan's friends used to bring women with them. I thought they were their wives. It amused me to see how oddly they were dressed – in high-heeled shoes, and very short gold skirts, with their hair tied in a strange way.

Hasan said that was how people dressed in cities. I didn't know any big cities, so I believed him.

Now I can see how naïve I was. But I so badly wanted to believe Hasan really was a good man that I was capable of convincing myself of anything to avoid disrupting this dream.

But one evening Hasan disrupted the dream by ordering me to go to bed with one of his friends. When I refused, he knocked out my teeth.

Skirt

I realised that Hasan's friends had gradually been grooming me. Unfortunately, by now it was too late. First they had taught me to drink alcohol, and later to take drugs. Later still I had become addicted to those drugs.

But above all Hasan had entirely cut me off from the world outside. I had no job, no family and no friends. When Hasan's friend raped me, I had nowhere to run. I didn't even have the strength to run away. They started taking more and more liberties. Finally they dressed me in a short gold skirt, tied my hair strangely and took me to Kayseri, to a meeting like the ones at our house.

Drugs

They shut me in a brothel in a strange city. When I refused to work, they hit me, or didn't give me any drugs. You know the way a dog howls? I howled a hundred times more than that.

I worked like that for over eleven years. I only managed to escape a year ago. I can't talk about those eleven years yet, but I can tell you how I escaped.

Smart gentleman

I ran away for the first time after a month. I went walking down the street, trying to find someone I could trust. So I'm on the look-out, and along comes a very smart gentleman. I went up to him and said I'd just escaped from a brothel, where they'd hit me and raped me. The smart gentleman got very upset. 'Get back to your place, you whore!' he screamed.

And I went back.

They took me all over Turkey – Antalya, Malatya, Konya, Mersin. I can't remember all the cities anymore. Like this, the pimps in those places had new girls every two weeks, and they didn't have to pay any fees for us, because we never worked in the same place for an entire month.

One time they took me to Antalya. There was only meant to be one man, but there were six. They put a gun to my head. I told them about my minders, but they just laughed.

Not long after, someone killed a girl I'd worked with, and I ran away again. I was helped by a soldier, who took me off into the mountains, to his family. But they found me and beat me senseless. They said that if I ran away one more time they would kill me.

Operation

In 2005 I had an operation – women's matters. After the operation the doctor came and asked me accusingly: 'Why don't you want to have children?' And I said: 'What do you mean?' 'Well, you've just had your fallopian tubes cut!'

I'd been walled in. It turned out it was cheaper to have them cut than to pay for the occasional abortion. They didn't tell me what was happening. They did the same thing to all the girls.

That was when I decided I was either going to run away, or die.

Supermarket

I grabbed at the first chance. There was this young lad, I think he was rather in love with me. He paid extra just to be with me and to talk to me.

'I can see the pain in your eyes,' he said. I went to pieces, and I told him everything. He promised to get me out.

In Turkey we have a television programme where journalists intervene in difficult situations, and he called them up.

A few weeks later a journalist came to see me, pretending to be a client. He was festooned in cameras, and he'd brought a contract in a shopping bag, which I signed. It said they couldn't guarantee my safety. He asked if I knew I could get killed. I said I would rather die than go on living like that.

He said they'd have to record my attempt to escape.

The next day I asked the boss to let me go shopping. As a minder he gave me a guy who had killed three people before then. In the supermarket I tried to run away from him. He caught me by the till, hit me in the face and threw me on my back – then shoved me into the car.

When we drove up to the brothel, the television people and the police were already there. He tried to force his way through the cordon, but he failed.

That was in spring 2006. I was free. I felt like a bird whose cage has been opened, but which hasn't got the strength to fly anymore.

Photos

Saliha shows me photos of her daughters on her phone, then a picture of her father. That's all she has left of her relatives; none of them will speak to her now. They're trying to forget about her, as if she were never alive.

One of the reasons why she is standing for parliament is to recover her dignity, and to show her relatives that she is still worth something.

Headscarf

Along with the television people, my younger daughter was waiting for me. She had a present for me – a headscarf like the ones religious women wear. At the brothel they advertised me as the girl with the loveliest hair. I had long hair, down to my waist. *From her wallet Saliha takes out a picture of herself in those days. There are some red streaks spoiling her raven-black hair, but even so it looks fabulous.*

My daughter put the headscarf on me and said: 'Wear it, so no one will ever mess up your lovely hair again.'

Greece

My older brother lives in Greece. While he was at work, his wife recorded the programme about my rescue. 'Do you know that woman?' she asked him. 'No, I don't,' he said, and went out.

When he came back, she explained to him that he couldn't ignore the facts, and that he should help me. They sent me an invitation, but I couldn't get a visa. But I thought there was a better life waiting for me in Greece, so I decided to get there at any price. I crossed the border illegally and hitchhiked to my brother's place. It turned out he was in a tricky situation himself – he was out of work and his debts were increasing. He always had something to complain about.

His wife gave me twenty euros for a ticket home. At the border the customs officer slapped a 600-euro fine on me because I didn't have an entry stamp. I don't know how I'm going to pay it.

Cousin

I returned to Adana, my home town, and went to live with my cousin. He received me very kindly – too kindly. I had been through too much not to be cautious.

My cousin invited me out for supper. He said I needed to find a man, and that I must appear in public. Meanwhile he was calling all the pimps in the city, trying to sell me. He wanted one billion old lira for me – 50,000 euros. Then he went down to one-third of that price, and then to a thousand dollars.

In Adana none of them wanted me, because they knew I covered my head. A woman in a headscarf prompts respect, not desire. So then he started calling other cities.

One day a strange man phoned. He introduced himself as 'a family friend': 'Tell your brother not to keep bothering me. I really don't want you! Tell him to stop calling!'

Daughters

My older daughter is twenty now. She wanted to become a policewoman. I had to tell her about my past myself, otherwise she'd have found out from somebody else.

Ever since, she doesn't want to know me. Her boyfriend dumped her because of me, and they wouldn't have her in the police either. She lives with her father; he refers to me as 'that woman'.

The worst thing is that she has turned my younger daughter against me. She was a real support to me, but now she doesn't want to know me either. Lately she sent me a text message which said: 'People are saying I came from the womb of a whore. If I were you, I'd rather not be alive.'

Ayşe and Saliha have been holding hands all this time. There are tears pouring straight down their cheeks without trickling around the freckles and dimples anymore. One by one they drip onto the headscarf, onto the table, onto the cup.

As Saliha talks about her daughters, Ayşe hugs her with all her might.

'It's all right now, darling,' she says. 'You don't have to say any more. Now it's my turn.'

ayşe tükrükçü's story

Ayşe's hair is dyed red and she has a defiant ring in her nose, with a scattering of freckles around it. She speaks confidently, but the whole time she never lets go of Cennet – a doll that looks like a baby.

I don't like this sort of conversation. You'd have to cut me in half to know what I've really got inside – what's in my head, eyes and heart. There's no other way you'll ever understand me. But anyway, let's give it a try.

Documents

Our biggest problem is the fact that the past keeps trailing after us. Look, here are my documents – employment certificates from brothels in Mersin, Adana and Gaziantep. I had to pay a hundred dollars for each one, and I need them in order to try for any kind of job. But if I apply for a job and come along with documents like these, who's going to employ me?

All Turkish men go to brothels, but none of them will employ a former prostitute.

Look at this picture on the wall. That woman was a prostitute for forty years, but the brothel only paid her pension for three. In her old age she had to scavenge scraps out of dustbins.

It's even hard for us to get a plot in a graveyard.

The worst thing is that prostitution is legal in Turkey, so if you run away, the police will take you straight back to the brothel. They refuse to listen when you tell them somebody beat you up and raped you. In the evening the same policemen come there as your customers, and they get a discount from the boss for having found you.

Glass

I was born not far from Gaziantep, a city surrounded by lovely green pistachio groves.

When I was two, my parents went abroad to Germany, leaving me behind with my grandmother. They didn't come back for me until I was seven.

After all those years, my mother and father were strangers to me. The first day after I arrived in Germany my father was at work. My mother said: 'Let's prepare food for him'. He came home, and didn't say a word to me. He tried the soup we'd made, then took hold of the tablecloth by two corners and overturned the whole lot onto the floor – because it was too greasy.

He'd beat up my mother, then she'd hit my aunt, and my aunt would hit me. My mother would beat us simply because the washing machine had gone wrong, or a glass had broken. My father was an alcoholic. My brother was already having psychiatric treatment then.

Knife

My grandmother didn't know how to read or write, so two years later she recorded a tape and sent it to my father. She asked him to send me back to her, so that I could look after her in her old age.

In Germany the Berlin Wall was still standing. In my home village in Turkey nobody had a television set. I was nine years old. My uncle was a taxi driver in Antalya, a large resort on the Mediterranean. He told my grandmother I'd be useful to him during the tourist season. He took me and his daughter to cook for him.

After a few days I woke up in the night drenched in sweat. There was something crawling up my legs! I thought it was mice, but it wasn't – it was my uncle's hand. I started to scream, and then he stuck a knife in my back.

Ayşe folds back her shirt and shows me a scar – her uncle's knife went in just below her left shoulder blade.

There was a wooden parquet floor in that room – I've hated wooden parquet floors ever since. For three and a half months, night after night he kept touching me, and he made his daughter watch. He threatened that if I ever told anyone, he'd do something worse to me.

Sunflower

When the season ended, we went back to Gaziantep. I was afraid of everything. Whenever guests came to our house, I would run away – especially from men.

My grandmother asked about the wound, but I didn't answer. All I said was that I wanted to go and see my aunt in the mountains.

My grandmother was a wise woman. She didn't protest, she just got some food ready for me, including a very big dried sunflower head, the biggest one I'd ever seen.

But all my life I've had this habit, every time I'm finally on the straight, of doing something stupid. I started shelling the sunflower seeds, so I wasn't paying attention, and the bus left without me. Someone said I could take the next one, so I boarded it, and ended up in Izmir – four hundred kilometres from home. I thought I seemed to have gone too far, but someone gave me a sesame ring, and somebody else started talking to me, and it was nice, so I travelled onwards.

In Izmir I ended up at the police. The policemen were kind too. The police chief took me home for the night. His wife gave me some soup and played games with me. I was with them for over a week, and I was hoping I'd stay there.

But one day my uncle and his wife were waiting for me at the police station. As soon as I saw them, I stopped caring if I went on living or died.

Polo neck

My uncle sent me back to Germany. He told my father it was impossible to put up with me. My father greeted me with such a beating that I couldn't sit down for a week – just because I'd burned the rice.

It was summer, very hot, and I went to school in a polo-necked top. The teacher began to suspect something. She followed me to the toilet, pulled up my top, and saw that my whole body was covered in bruises. They did a full examination and took my father to court.

I ended up in a refuge for young people. My four years in that refuge were the best years of my life.

Fingernail

Only four years later did my mother come to visit me. My family didn't want to know me. They called me *kara kız*, the black girl – bringing shame.

My mother said they were leaving for Turkey, and that I had a week to decide if I was going with them or not. She had a head injury.

My first thought? I'm staying here! I'd seen on television that there was a military regime in Turkey and I didn't want to go there, but then I'd be left all alone. My family and I are like a finger and a fingernail – apparently separate objects, but all part of the same thing.

In the end we didn't go back to Turkey, and my father learned how to hit us without it showing. So I ran away, and spent a year living on the street.

At the same time they wanted to marry my uncle's daughter, Sengül – the girl I'd shared a room with – to my mentally ill brother. The doctor said marriage might help him. There was no other candidate, so they wanted to marry him to his cousin.

Except that she couldn't get a visa.

'Go and fetch her, and I'll forgive you everything,' my father told me. I was tempted to ask which of us really had something to forgive the other, but I bit my tongue.

Plums

So I went to Turkey. I badly wanted to have a family – a real one. Then I met a boy whose name was Hasan. He wasn't good-looking or ugly, but what mattered to me was that within his family everyone treated everyone else with respect.

A few weeks after the wedding I fell pregnant.

My mother-in-law didn't like me. One day I got a craving for some green plums, which in Turkey are a delicacy. I was in my fifth month by then, so it was one of those pregnancy cravings. My mother-in-law said I wouldn't get any, to which I replied that I'd tell my husband everything. We began to argue, and her other son took his mother's side. He pushed me out of the house and I fell down some steps.

I lay there for three hours. It was raining very hard. Only towards evening did a girlfriend take me to the toilet, where I felt something come flooding out of me.

In the morning, it turned out to have been a baby boy.

My husband wasn't on my side. I told him that thanks to him anyone could piss on our child now, and I filed for a divorce.

Tailor

In Gaziantep I met a tailor, who fell in love with me, or so at least he said. All my life I'd never seen anyone sew that badly. 'How can he make a living out of that?' I thought.

Then it turned out the tailor was brilliant at stitching up people.

We had a religious wedding, before an imam, and we had a few months to wait for a civil one. But the tailor had other plans. I was young, pretty and entirely alone – ideal to be sold to a brothel. Especially as a religious wedding has no real significance at all, neither for the police nor in any official capacity.

However, the tailor couldn't just walk in off the street and say: 'Here's my wife, give me some money'. He had to formalise things.

He started with a certificate from the police stating that I was a whore. How did he get it? Very craftily. He told me to put on a mini skirt and some make-up. 'Darling,' I said, 'you know this is a small town. People will start saying things about me behind my back.' But he insisted. In Turkey you don't argue with a man.

On the way we had sex in the car. About a quarter of an hour later he told me to wait at a petrol station. 'Get out of the car,' he said. I tried to argue, but it was impossible. So I got out and waited; meanwhile he called the police to say there was a whore at the petrol station. They came and took me away. They did tests, which showed that I had just had intercourse.

In court his friend testified that he had paid me for sex too. The court sentenced me to twenty-three days in prison, and the police gave my husband the certificate, from which it appeared that Ayşe Tükrükçü was a prostitute.

I thought the whole story was a mistake. I never heard the witness statements, because nobody took me into the interview room. Besides, even if I had heard them, I wouldn't have understood. I'd spent most of my life in Germany, and at the time I didn't know Turkish at all well. On top of that, my tailor kept confusing me, because he was always coming to the prison and telling me how much he loved me.

When I came out, he gave me a document to sign from the police. He said it was for the civil wedding, so I didn't even read it. I wanted to be free as quickly as possible.

What I had signed was an agreement to work in a brothel in Gaziantep. With this bit of paper, now he could sell me.

Fish tank

The day after I came out of prison the tailor took me to a strange place. There was a large fish tank by the entrance, and there were girls standing on the stairs in strange poses.

We sat down at a small table and the tailor said he had to leave me here for a few months. He said I'd do some work, and then we'd get married, just as we'd planned.

'What are you thinking of?!' I shouted and tried to leave. Then he hit me. 'Just remember you're not to make love with anyone the way you do with me!' he quipped as a parting shot.

It was a large brothel, the biggest in the city. There was always a policeman standing by the door, making sure the customers were at least eighteen years old. After work he used to come in himself. There was access for an ambulance, a kitchen, and a large bar.

The tailor got 1,500 dollars for me.

Cigarette

I dug in my heels and said I wasn't going to work. The guy who stood in the doorway gave me a severe beating, and then they raped me. They wouldn't give me anything to eat or drink. I might have held out for longer if they'd at least let me have a cigarette.

But they didn't, so after ten days I started working.

In Turkey prostitution is legal. Supposedly this helps to protect women. Maybe that's true, but no one ever checks! In those days nobody used condoms. I only saw the doctor once every few years because he'd done a deal with the boss and he used to sign our health booklets all in one go, without examining us. That doctor only ever appeared when someone had to have an abortion. After the abortion you got a red armband for a few days, which meant you had the right not to work.

On other days the armband was black. Then I had to serve thirty men. But if a thirty-first came along, there was no mercy.

If I was bleeding, they gave me tampons.

One day the girls from another city didn't arrive on time, and I had to serve seventy-six men. Everybody came there – policemen, officials, even dustmen. Two men died in my bed of heart attacks.

Axe

A sight I will never forget as long as I live is Özlam and her cut-off head. Her brother had sold her to the brothel, but when she fell pregnant, she insisted on having the baby. So the pimp called her brother to get him to return the money.

The brother was terribly upset, and came along with an axe. When I went into the parlour, Özlam was lying on the sofa and her head was half a metre away.

Cake
We're watching a film that's more than ten years old. There are at least a dozen women sitting on small chairs. They're all dressed up with their hair done, looking rather unnatural. Another clip shows a bride in a white dress, sitting next to a bridegroom, who has a mop of black wavy hair. The next one shows the bride cutting a large cake. Someone is trying to dance, but it looks ridiculous.

That was my third wedding – the wedding of my dreams. I had a band, a four-tier cake with a bride and groom on top, and a bridesmaid. I'd seen a cake like that as a child at my cousin's wedding.

The only thing missing was the children who usually carry the veil. And there was nobody from my family.

My fiancé was called Mahmut. He was a customer of mine who'd kept on coming to see me, until finally he proposed. At the brothel they said I could leave if I paid my debts. The way it works is that they subtract money from your pay for food, lodging, laundry and electricity, and towards the end of the month it would turn out they didn't owe me anything, but I owed them. I had paid them enough to buy a flat and a good car. They spread the debt out for me in instalments, and I spent several years paying it off. But I was free!

Television
All the television channels showed our wedding. 'Ayşe and Mahmut, the couple from the brothel,' wrote the newspapers.

When you come out of a place like that, you have to learn

to live all over again. You have to forget about all the abortions and the bleeding, and try to remember how to cook and clean. Mahmut did not prove to be a good husband. He used to spend all day watching television. I felt as if the TV set was his wife, not I.

After a month he hit me for the first time. I didn't wait for him to do it again. I ran away.

Cennet

Cennet, the doll's name, means 'heaven' in Turkish. Ayşe sits it on her knees, strokes its head and kisses its hand, then puts a little headscarf on it. No, she is not acting like a lunatic who thinks the doll is a child. It is that for her Cennet is a symbol of all the children she might have had. In every picture in every newspaper Ayşe wants to appear with Cennet.

'Whatever may happen to you in life / you'll end up dead and buried. / Flowers will bloom on the spot, / and trees will bear their fruit,' *wrote Ayşe in a poem which she included in her election leaflet.*

'What's hardest for me is to close my eyes,' she says, when we meet again after the elections. 'It all comes back in my dreams. The worst thing is that I have too much time. Now that the interviews and the campaign are over, I'm sitting at home alone again, and that's when I remember it all. Once again I have no one but Cennet.'

epilogue

Jointly, Ayşe and Saliha won almost a thousand votes, which isn't much, not enough to get into parliament.

However, their stories appeared in plenty of newspapers and on television shows. They prompted debate, and the press began to call for greater control of brothels. 'Their stories made me feel ashamed. They put all Turkey to shame,' wrote a well-known commentator. 'We cannot take tax money from these ladies, and then leave them to their fate when they're in dire poverty,' wrote another. 'Turkish men are supposed to think of women as sacred. So I ask: where are the people who go to brothels when former prostitutes are dying of hunger? Don't these women deserve respect?' concluded another.

In Turkey the selling of women – wives, sisters and friends – is a serious epidemic. Research conducted in Diyarbakır, which has a population of one million, showed that in the course of a year in this city alone at least four hundred families are supported in this way.

abraham's carp

1

'SHALL I TELL YOU A SECRET?' he asks, pointing a finger at me which has lost half its nail.

He's wearing checked trousers and an Indian-style shirt, and has stringy, shoulder-length hair – not exactly a tangled mat, but more like dreadlocks. He accosts me at the mosque in Şanlıurfa, a holy place where the prophet Abraham was born. He stinks like an old dog, one of his shoes is full of holes and the other has no laces.

'What do I care about some hippy's secrets?' I think. But I've nothing better to do. It's noon, baking hot, and I feel as if my head is in an oven. So I'm sitting in the shade of a tree and – good luck to him – go ahead, I'm all ears.

'I am Jesus Christ, the Son of God,' he whispers. 'Buy me some cigarettes.'

I buy him a packet of red Marlboros. Jesus inhales, relaxes, and asks if I know the history of his city. I do, but he tells me anyway how the soldiers of King Nimrod – the man who tried to build the tower of Babel – came to kill Abraham (here they call him Ibrahim). And how Allah changed the soldiers into fish. And although, according to the historians, Nimrod and

Abraham lived in completely different eras, I don't interrupt my personal Jesus.

2

To this day the soldiers who were changed into fish are still swimming about in a pool near Abraham's cave. There are no fish like them anywhere in the world. They only have to see the shadow of a man, and at once they leap out of the water, furiously slap their tails against its surface, push, jump on each other's backs and tug at each other's fins. They look like one huge creature with a thousand heads, having a fight with itself. Their scales shine in the sunlight like armour. But today they are no longer fighting for King Nimrod's mercy – today the battle is for a bit of bread or wheat from the pilgrims.

'No Muslim will touch the flesh of these fish. He would die instantly,' says Christ, and touches me for a bit of change, this time for a pilaf, rice with chicken, which a street vendor is touting.

I give it to him. After all, it was He who said: 'For I was hungry and you fed me'. And as Christ runs after the vendor, I think about all the messiahs I have come across here in Turkey.

3

In 2002 Dursun Ali Bacıoğlu, an engineer from the Black Sea port of Trabzon, declared himself to be Christ and stood for parliament. Only sixty-seven people voted for him. When a local paper ran an article about him with the headline *Fake Messiah Loses Election*, he sued it. For lack of proof of his messianic mission, the court dismissed his suit.

In 2006 another messiah arrived in Ankara from the town of Gebze, a place famous for the fact that it is thought to be where

Hannibal committed suicide. He brought with him a hunting rifle, a pistol and a knife, and made straight for the headquarters of the chief of general staff, where he was arrested.

In 2007 another one hijacked a plane from Istanbul to Gaziantep, Turkey's pistachio-nut capital. He demanded an appearance on state television, because he wanted to announce that the end of the world was coming next week. However, he didn't get his wish and never made his announcement.

Until recently the most popular of the Turkish messiahs was Hasan Mezarcı, former deputy to the Meclis (the Turkish parliament) and religious radical. With a storm of greying hair and a thick beard, he wears a golden coat and is decked in strings of beads and necklaces as he prophesies the end of the world on the front pages of the major Turkish newspapers, and tells Christian churches to swap their icons of Christ for photographs of him. His parents have disowned him, whereas his wife has publicly accused anyone who doubts her husband's messianic mission of being a cretin.

4

Some Muslims believe the messiah will be the prophet Isa, in other words Jesus. Others speak of a missing imam, who will appear close to Judgement Day. However, he is not such an important figure in Islam as in Christianity. So how did the Turks come up with the idea of seeking him among themselves?

They were probably inspired by Sabbatai Zevi, the first messiah to become famous in Turkey. He was born in the seventeenth century in Smyrna, today Izmir, where for many years he studied the cabbala.

In 1648 the devout Jews were expecting the world to end. They regarded the massacres carried out by Khmelnytsky's Cossacks when they attacked the Polish Republic as a sign from heaven and 'the birth pangs of the Messiah'.* When Zevi announced that he was God's chosen one, thousands of people believed him.

But when the end of the world failed to occur for the next three years, the Jews drove him out of Smyrna. Sabbatai spent at least ten years wandering about Turkey, until from another flash of insight he learned that the end of the world had not been cancelled, but merely postponed until 1666.

In May 1665 the prophet Nathan of Gaza confirmed that Zevi was the messiah, and proclaimed that any day now the Turkish sultan would become his servant. Soon after, the messiah found out about a Jewish woman who had miraculously survived Khmelnytsky's massacres. Her name was Sarah, she lived in the Italian city of Livorno, where she worked as a prostitute, and claimed that she was going to be the wife of the messiah.

Sabbatai had once had a vision which told him that his wife would be a woman of dubious reputation. When he heard the story of Sarah, he gave orders for her to be brought to him at once.

According to the historians of Sabbatianism, the former prostitute's beauty and charisma, as well as the marketing value of this story, won the messiah many new supporters.

Early in 1666 some Turkish soldiers arrested Sabbatai Zevi and shut him in a fortress in Gallipoli. In September Zevi went to Edirne to be interrogated. On seeing the messiah being led into the sultan's court, thousands of local Jews cheered in the belief that Sabbatai was going to convert the ruler to Judaism.

But things turned out quite differently.

---

* Quotations and information on the activities of Sabbatai Zevi and Jakub Frank are from a book by Jan Doktór, *Śladami mesjasz-apostaty. Żydowskie ruchy mesjańskie w XVII i XVIII wieku a problem konwersji* ('Evidence of the messiah-apostate: Jewish messianic movements in the 17th and 18th century and the issue of conversion'), Wrocław, 1998.

5

We don't know exactly what happened at Sabbatai's interrogation. The Turkish sources say he was questioned in the presence of Mehmed IV himself – the man who waged ferocious war against the Poles, and less than twenty years later sent the Grand Vizier Kara Mustafa to Vienna. They also say that the interrogators threatened to cut off his head, and told him to prove he could perform miracles: 'Stripped naked, he was to serve the court archers as a firing target. If his body resisted the arrows and did not sustain any wounds, the sultan would promise to declare him the Messiah.'

Sabbatai probably didn't believe his body could resist arrows. In any case, he had no intention of taking the risk, so he meekly admitted that 'there is no god but Allah, and Mohammed is His prophet', and emerged from the interrogation as a fully entitled Muslim. The imams hoped that the conversion of the Jewish messiah would help them to win thousands of his co-religionists over to Islam.

And so it was – all over the country, crowds of Jews began to adopt Islam.

This was the start of a conversion which to this day stirs strong emotions in Turkey. For although he accepted Islam, Sabbatai did not dissociate himself from Judaism or from his messianic mission. For whole centuries his followers officially considered themselves to be Muslims, but secretly met and prayed as before. The Turks called then *dönme* – converts. To this day they are regarded as crypto-Jews who only care about their own interests and who lurk in corners plotting how to do harm to Turkey. There are hundreds of conspiracy theories doing the rounds in Turkey which claim it is the *dönme* who actually rule the country. Everyone comes under suspicion: Atatürk, because he came from Salonica (now Thessaloniki), the city where Sabbatai lived after being exiled from Izmir;

Nazım Hikmet, because his grandfather was governor of the same city; and prime minister Erdoğan, because he wants to strengthen Islam, but an Islamic Turkey is a weak Turkey, and a weak Turkey is desired by all the Jews in the world.

Some commentators can't help wondering why it is that in a country where there are practically no Jews at all the citizens are capable of sniffing out Jewish conspiracies at every step of the way.

6

In Izmir a guide once showed me Sabbatai Zevi's house in one of the side streets. He was a good guide of the older generation. His name was Ahmet, and he lamented the fact that few people knew this place. He did, because his grandmother's house had once stood 300 metres further on.

Sabbatai's house is in a pitiful state. The upper storeys have collapsed along with the roof, revealing in the process the remains of some old frescoes.

'*Dönme* still come here to this day,' Ahmet told me, yet there was no quest for conspiracies or unwholesome sensation-seeking in this remark, more like sympathy. 'They light candles and perform some sort of rituals. Oh, look, here are some marks left by the candles,' he said, pointing them out as we wandered round the house, glancing left and right to make sure nothing was going to come down on us. 'Fifty years ago my grandmother used to see more than a hundred of them here,' he added. 'I occasionally see just two old women. Apparently the city wants to demolish this house and build a park here. They'll probably succeed. The local Jews hate Sabbatai, and the *dönme* are afraid to stick their necks out.'

7

Sabbatai Zevi's mission had wide resonance among the Polish Jews too. This was inevitable – in those days Poland shared a border with Turkey. The city of Kamieniec Podolski (now Kamyanets-Podilsky in Ukraine) regularly changed hands, and the Polish Republic and the Ottoman Porte had the reputation of being the most tolerant countries in Europe. Jews from the territory of today's Ukraine went to Smyrna, Salonica and Constantinople to study the Torah and the cabbala. Jewish Turks also frequented Poland, if only as merchants.*

One of Sabbatai's Polish pupils, Jakub Frank, was born in 1726 and also declared himself to be the messiah. Persecuted by the rabbis, he and his followers adopted Christianity, first in Lwów (now Lviv, Ukraine) and later in Warsaw.

Like the Ottoman imams, the Catholic bishops believed Frank's baptism was the first step towards the souls of all the Jews. But when it transpired that in spite of his conversion Frank still regarded himself as the messiah, he ended up as a prisoner at the Jasna Góra Monastery.

8

As I bring all this back to mind, my personal Jesus Christ from Şanlıurfa is polishing off a pilaf, and smiling broadly. I think a good psychiatrist would have quite a job with him. But it doesn't really matter; these days they say the same thing about Sabbatai Zevi, yet thousands of people followed him.

---

* For more on this topic, see: Rachel Elior, *The Mystical Origins of Hasidism*, translated by Shalom Carmy, Portland, 2006. This book also describes how the Hassidic movement was inspired by Sabbatianism and Frankism, the movement founded by Sabbatai Zevi's pupil, Jakub Frank.

We are in a land where it was enough to lose a sheep in the mountains for a new religion to be born. Except that today this land is building roads, putting up shops and recording pretty good economic growth. Neither hijacking planes nor wearing golden costumes is adequate anymore. These days a messiah will really have to try very hard if he's going to catch the attention of the Turks.

the assassin from apricot city

1

AT THE TOWN CENTRE there are several benches painted green. Next to them there's a statue of the former mayor İsmet İnönü, who was a comrade-in-arms of Atatürk and had the dubious pleasure of being born here in Malatya.

Why dubious? Because this is a dump like no other. If it weren't for football – the local team, Malatyaspor, plays in the first league, and the stadium even has AstroTurf – you could die of boredom here.

And in summer there are also the apricots. The town is surrounded by hectares and hectares of orchards, with millions of small trees in them. The fruit goes all over Europe. The summer here is green and orange, with the scent and flavour of apricots.

The winter is very different – nothing happens in Malatya then. There are no tourists, but there are heaps of dirty snow lying in the streets, and the benches under the mayor's statue are deserted. It's bloody cold – being 900 metres above sea level takes its toll. In winter the locals are dejected, bad-tempered and rarely emerge from their houses.

1958
In just this sort of hostile winter, in the village of Hekimhan outside Malatya, Mehmet Ali Ağca is born. His parents live in a modest wooden cottage. His father has problems finding work, and often turns to drink.

A few months after the birth of little Mehmet, Father Karol Wojtyła becomes auxiliary bishop of Krakow. He is thirty-eight, and is the youngest member of the Polish Catholic hierarchy. By this point he has already acknowledged the Virgin Mary as his patron saint, and *Totus Tuus* ('All Yours') as his guiding motto.

2

In Malatya there are shops where the only items on offer are apricots prepared in a thousand different ways. This must be the only city of its kind in the world. Best of all are the apricots stuffed with nuts: walnuts, hazelnuts and pistachios.

The owners of these shops utter the name of Ali Ağca with particular reverence. They argue over which of them was better friends with him.

'I went to junior school with him,' says the first.

'I sold water at the railway station with him,' says the second.

I don't entirely believe them – I get the impression half the population of Malatya boasts of being acquainted with Ağca.

Only the third salesman doesn't brag, because he is from Diyarbakır. But his kids play at being Ağca with the others – one child fires a stick at another. None of them wants to be the Pope. They all want to be Ağca. And when their team runs out onto the AstroTurf, for years the Malatyaspor fans have sung: 'Long live Malatya, long live the Pope, we love you Ali Aaaaağcaaa!'

I buy a few boxes of wrinkled apricots and enter a courtyard, one of thousands. The cab drivers come here to wash their lemon-yellow taxis. They're smoking cigarettes and gossiping, and they greet me, because a foreigner is not an everyday sight around here.

I wave back and press a round door buzzer – the one next to the name Ağca.

1966

Ağca's father dies. Apparently towards the end of his life he was never sober at all, and beat the boy's mother. Eight-year-old Mehmet Ali becomes head of the family. He has to work to support his mother and siblings, so he sells water and sweets on trains.

His mother is unconditionally in love with him. She believes her son will go very far. Perhaps he'll be a doctor? Or even a professor? Whoever he becomes, the world is sure to hear about him.

Meanwhile, by now Karol Wojtyła is the Archbishop of Krakow and a leading figure in the Polish episcopate. A year later he becomes Poland's second cardinal, after Stefan Wyszyński.

3

Adnan Ağca is the spitting image of his brother, except that his hair is still dark – Mehmet Ali has turned entirely grey. He greets me at the door and leads me into the main room. He's wearing a dark sweater gone bobbly with age, and cheap mules of the KicKars knock-off brand.

'My brother doesn't know about this flat. We moved here from Hekimhan when he was already in an Italian prison. Allah, Allah, my God, how many years it is now!'

His sister Fatma is sitting in the corner, next to a small pot-bellied stove – that's the warmest spot. She's watching me, but as soon as I glance in her direction she drops her gaze. She's wearing a Muslim headscarf.

'But we're not particularly religious,' explains Adnan. 'At Kurban Bayramı, the most important festival, we try to give the poor at least a chicken. Islam is very sensitive about alms. It is one of the most important commandments. But we rarely go to Friday *namaz*.'

There are also some uncles at home, Ali and Muhammed. They have come to visit, to get warm and have a chat. There are some kids here too: three of Adnan's, and three of Fatma's. I have brought them some classic Polish candy, a box of *Ptasie mleczko* ('Bird's milk') sweets and some plums in chocolate, but they're shy of me and are giggling in the hall.

I place my right hand on my chest and bow politely towards the younger of the Ağca brothers. Thank you for agreeing to talk to me. For years he hasn't let any journalists in. Just before me, he refused a television crew from Brazil, though apparently they stood freezing outside his house for two days.

Adnan returns my bow. Yes, it's true, he doesn't like hacks.

'They write rubbish about my brother,' he says, nodding. 'I say he sleeps peacefully, and they say that he has nightmares. I say he dreams of peace and quiet, they say he's going to write books and act in films. But you are from the Pope's country.' Adnan Ağca gives me a solemn look. 'The Pope never refused us, so how could I refuse you? Sit down with us and ask what you want – you are our friend,' he adds, and smiles.

1976

Mehmet Ali Ağca graduates from teacher-training school in Malatya and goes to college in Ankara. There, following in the footsteps of thousands of other boys, he falls into the clutches of a terrorist group. Turkey is steeped in anarchy. Left-wing extremists are fighting against the right. According to the late Claire Sterling, an American author who wrote some excellent books about

Ağca and about terrorism, in those days someone was killed by extremists in Turkey on average once an hour. The right-wing extreme – including the Grey Wolves, Ağca's organisation – dreams of a Greater Turkey stretching all the way to Mongolia, the land of the True Turks, free of left-wing influences.

The left-wing extreme, inspired by the USSR, wants closer ties between Turkey and its neighbour the USSR and the realisation of communist ideals on the Bosporus.

Both are dependent on dealing in drugs and weapons. The smuggling runs across Bulgaria, as a result of which the Bulgarian secret service has an influence on the terrorists – both left-wing and right-wing.

Ağca is ideally cut out to be a terrorist – he is capable, hardworking and hasn't a penny to his name. He is quick to learn.

A year later, in 1977, he goes to Palestinian camps in Syria for training. In 1978 he moves from Ankara to Istanbul. Never once does he show up at college.

That same year Karol Wojtyła becomes Pope and takes the name John Paul II.

4

We sit and slurp our tea.

In view of their age, the noisiest slurpers are the uncles. Both of them have big, bushy moustaches that look stuck on and – as befits those of patriarchal age – they don't say much. They just listen, nodding approvingly now and then.

'Mehmet Ali was a very good child,' Adnan tells me, and as the uncles remember him like that too, they nod their heads like the black plaster figures coins are thrown into in village churches. 'He never got into a fight with anyone, he never quarrelled. Those murderers exploited his good nature. They exploited our poverty. My brother is a good brother and a good son, a good person. He never wished anybody any harm,' he adds, and the uncles' heads fully agree with him.

The terrorist who shot at the Pope never wished anybody any harm? It's hard for me to believe that, but all right, if that's how they want it. I ask some questions about Ağca's childhood and youth.

While I'm asking, the uncles keep very still, listening carefully and weighing every word precisely. When it turns out I'm asking about the young Ağca's interests, about his girlfriends, jobs, plans and dreams, the uncles' heads move vertically, and that means approval.

Girlfriends? 'He never had any. They didn't interest him,' replies Adnan.

Work? 'He always worked hard. He helped his mother, brother and sister.'

Plans? 'He wanted to be a teacher, to have a wife, a house and children. He likes children very much.'

Dreams? 'He used to write poetry, he wanted to be a poet. No, none of them have survived. The police took everything.'

But when I ask about the Grey Wolves, terrorism and his first assassinations, the uncles' heads stop nodding. They don't like that sort of question. They swap glances, put the tips of their tongues to the roofs of their mouths and criticise me with low tut-tuts. Adnan is tut-tutting in the same way.

The Grey Wolves? 'My brother was exploited by them. He is a good person. He never wished anyone any harm.'

The camp in Syria? 'I don't know anything about that.'

The killings? 'He was exploited. Why should he kill anyone? He wasn't interested in politics, he never wished anyone any harm.'

The attempt on the Pope's life? 'He never wished anyone any harm. He loved the Pope like a father.'

So why did he shoot him? 'I don't know,' says Adnan, shrugging. 'My brother didn't know who the Pope was then.

It was all God's plan. Apart from which he was exploited...'

I'm not going to hold back.

'If he loved everyone and wished everybody well, why did he become a terrorist?' I ask irately.

Adnan has had enough of these questions. 'He was exploited, as I've already said. He never wished anyone any harm,' he repeats his refrain, and he'll go on repeating it *ad infinitum*. The tension between us reaches a dangerous upper limit – there's no point asking any more questions about Ali Ağca's past.

'And what sort of a person is he nowadays?' I ask instead. But at the same moment, the children who have been giggling in the hall until now finally dare to come steaming into the room. The first to run in is four-year-old Isa, the Turkish for Jesus, Adnan's son. Isa hops onto his father's knees and pulls his nose. After the little boy the girls come in: dark-haired Marie and blue-eyed Deniz (she gets it from her great-grandmother, who had blue eyes too).

Adnan hugs the kiddies. He tickles the girls and gives Isa's ear a tug. For several minutes he forgets all about his brother, the Pope, the Polish journalist and the questions he has had to keep answering for the past thirty years, though it wasn't he who shot at the Pope, it wasn't he who went to those camps in Syria, and it wasn't he who killed some Turkish journalists. For the moment all he can see is his darling kids, who are climbing on his head, yanking his hair and pulling at his bobbly sweater.

'What was I talking about?' he asks a little later, completely distracted. But by now I can't remember what I was going to ask him about either.

1ˢᵗ February 1979

The time is 7pm. Abdi İpekçi, a famous Turkish journalist, editor-in-chief of the popular daily *Milliyet*, a left-wing defender of human rights, is on his way home. He's nearly there – he just has to drive up the hill.

There's some snow on the ground in Istanbul and driving is difficult. Suddenly someone runs up to the car, takes out a gun and fires five shots. İpekçi dies instantly, and the killers get away.

For five long months they go unpunished. Nobody saw them, and the police don't even know where to look for them. One day, an anonymous informer unexpectedly calls police headquarters – the killer was Mehmet Ali Ağca, and right now he's at a restaurant on the Bosporus.

Ağca really is on the Bosporus. He doesn't offer the police the least resistance. He ends up in the closely guarded Kartal fortress prison in the suburbs of Istanbul. His trial begins.

A few months later, with the help of his terrorist associates Ağca escapes from prison in a military uniform.

He writes a letter in which he threatens to kill John Paul II, who is due to visit Turkey any day now: 'The Western imperialists... have sent John Paul, Commander of the Crusaders, to Turkey, disguised as a religious leader. If the visit... is not cancelled, I will not hesitate to kill the Pope. This was the one and only reason for my escape from prison.'

Nevertheless, the Pope comes to Istanbul. During his visit Ağca escapes to Bulgaria.

Soon after, John Paul II makes his first pilgrimage to Poland. He fills the hearts of his compatriots with hope, the result of which is the birth of Solidarity. This is probably when he signs his own death warrant – he is too dangerous for Moscow.

Ağca already knows he's going to take part in an important operation. Does he know he's going to shoot the Pope? Probably not. To cover their tracks, his handlers send him on a big trip – he goes to Iran, Sofia, Rome, Zurich, Vienna, Morocco, Milan and Tunisia. He writes a diary, in which he boasts of hiring a prostitute in Sofia and having sex with her in one of the churches. He goes about in camel-hair coats and wears a gold Rolex. He has a great deal of money, and also the reputation of being a brutal maniac. It would be hard to find a better candidate for assassinating the Pope.

5

Ever since Mehmet Ali has been in prison, in keeping with Turkish custom, Adnan has assumed his duties as head of the family. 'Only until my brother is released,' he stresses. In any case, whenever possible he asks him for advice. For instance, Mehmet Ali advised what names to give the children when they were born. It was he who wanted Adnan's son to be called Isa – Jesus, and his daughter Marie – Mary, and so it was.

The first time Adnan failed to ask his brother's advice was only a few weeks ago. He couldn't, so he made his own decision to take their gravely ill mother to hospital. Muzeyyen Ağca has diabetes and is dying.

'He might not have been able to bear it,' says Adnan. 'Our mother matters most of all to him. He'd give up his life for her. As a small boy he did everything to make sure she wouldn't have to work,' he explains. 'Then he used to send her money or presents from Ankara. When he was in prison, my mother and I went to Italy. It was hard, because that sort of trip costs a lot, and nobody helped us. But the Pope did not let us down. When he found out we were in Rome, he postponed all his meetings to talk to us. He said: "Mehmet Ali is my brother, and you are like a family for me".'

13th May 1981

Wearing a white shirt and a grey summer jacket, Ağca goes to Saint Peter's Square. He is carrying a Browning 9mm pistol bought in Vienna specially for this day. He is standing near the

Bronze Door, three metres away from the route the Pope is to take after his general audience.

Twenty metres away a brutal terrorist called Oral Çelik is waiting by a fountain; he is a friend of Ağca's from Malatya. He is wearing a leather jacket, jeans and trainers, and is carrying a Beretta 7.65mm pistol, and just in case, a fragmentation grenade.

At about 5pm the audience ends and the popemobile starts to go around Saint Peter's Square. As usual, the Pope greets the pilgrims, clasps their hands, and blesses the children. He is gradually coming nearer to Ağca.

At 5.17pm Ağca slowly raises his Browning and shoots. He hits the Pope in the stomach and elbow. The wound in the stomach could well have been fatal, but it isn't – the bullet misses the major organs by millimetres. The Pope is seriously wounded, and is bleeding, but he manages to survive. This is the first miracle to occur that day.

The second happens a little later on, when the Pope forgives his attacker.

Çelik manages to run off. To this day no one knows if he fired any shots, or if he didn't reach for his gun at all.

Ağca is caught by a brave nun, Sister Letizia, who holds onto him until the police arrive.

6

At an office on the second floor of a shabby tenement building on the outskirts of Istanbul there is a plaque on the door saying: 'Mustafa Demirbağ, Attorney'.

'I got this case rather by accident.' Demirbağ, who is Ali Ağca's lawyer, is wearing a smart black polo-necked top and a dark jacket. 'One day Adnan quarrelled with his brother's lawyers. He accused them of being so busy making careers for themselves on the back of Ağca that they had forgotten about the man himself.'

Demirbağ didn't want to take the case, but Adnan Ağca insisted. They agreed that before refusing, the lawyer would visit Mehmet Ali in prison.

'I was curious about the man,' he now relates. 'He's a living legend. I thought he was dangerous. I was afraid he could do me harm. I sat down in the visiting room. He came in, shook my hand, and gave me a timid smile. I thought he was very polite, embarrassed by the whole situation. When he asked if I would agree to conduct his case, I was already under his spell. I couldn't say no.'

Demirbağ's life took a 180-degree turn. The little-known lawyer suddenly began to give interviews and to attend recordings of television talk shows. He also started receiving text messages containing threats, so just in case, he bought a gun. But above all he started getting to know Ağca in person.

'I gathered up everything I could find about him. Eight big binders,' he says, and fetches three of them, as many as he can carry. 'I started going to the prison twice, sometimes as often as four times a week. I've been devoting my entire life to this case, all my free time, everything.'

What sort of a man is Ali Ağca? 'Wonderful, quite different from what you might read in the press. He's well-read, and fiendishly intelligent. If anyone ever tries to pull his strings for their own aims, it won't work. He can sense deceit instantly. But he's very amicable. Whenever we talk, he always looks me in the eye.'

What does he dream of? 'Peace and quiet. He wants to hide away somewhere quietly in the countryside, and live like that. Far away from it all.'

Are you friends? 'I try to keep a lawyer-client distance, but it really is difficult.' Demirbağ lights another cigarette. 'For many years no one talked to Ağca the way you talk to a friend: how are you doing, what are you reading, what were the league results, and that sort of thing. He had a great hunger for conversation. We have nice chats. That's all I can say.'

1983
Ağca is in an Italian prison. He is no longer counting on his associates to help him to escape, as before. He starts to testify, and grasses on his old terrorist pals, including the Grey Wolves.

In June, unknown perpetrators kidnap fifteen-year-old Emanuela Orlandi, daughter of a Vatican employee. They want to swap her for Ağca, but oddly, Ağca says he doesn't want to be released at all, and that he's doing fine in prison. He's afraid that if he comes out, his former associates will kill him. The girl has never been found to this day.

When his trial begins, he retracts all his earlier statements and declares himself to be the messiah. 'I am far greater than Charles Darwin and Sigmund Freud!' he shouts.

7

Rabia Özden Kazan refuses to meet with me.

'It's all too recent for me to talk about it,' she says. 'It still hurts too much.'

I manage to persuade her to give me a short interview over the phone. From pictures I know she is a beautiful woman with thick, dark eyebrows and hazel eyes. Like many women in the east of Turkey, she wears a black Muslim headscarf which covers her hair. She used to be Ali Ağca's fiancée, but they broke it off.

'I broke it off,' says the beautiful Rabia. 'It's hard to have a fiancé in prison. Especially a fiancé like that one,' she adds, sighing heavily.

Rabia is a journalist. A few years ago she went to do an interview with Ağca, which was how they met.

'I didn't know much about him,' she says. 'Just that he was a terrorist. I was expecting to meet a monster, but he turned out to be an engaging, sensitive man. Most men in Turkey think the best way to treat a woman is to play the tough guy, whereas Ağca is very warm and affectionate.

'Prison has made him much more mature than other men – he has a far better idea of what's important in life. And the most curious thing of all, you won't believe me, but Ali Ağca used to blush when we talked. He's shy!

'I could see at once that he liked me. I liked him too. He's very interesting, and instead of talking about terrorism we started talking about life. "Life is like a breadcrumb," he said, but he never explained what that meant, and I didn't dare ask.

'In an hour I'd told him all about myself, as if he were my best friend. A year later we were engaged.'

The idyll did not last long. News of the engagement leaked to the press, and journalists began to follow Rabia, phone her and write about their relationship. One of them wrote that she was a whore in the service of the Grey Wolves, and that Ağca's former associates were paying her to give him a bit of pleasure. He asked how come the giants of Turkish journalism had been begging to interview Ağca for six years and got nowhere, but Rabia Özden Kazan, writing for a marginal newspaper, had just walked into Istanbul's Kartal fortress as if it were a supermarket?

Apparently what hurt Rabia the most was that Ağca didn't deny it.

1983

On the second day of Christmas week, a black Mercedes with Vatican number plates drives through the gates of Italy's Rebibbia prison; John Paul II has come to visit the man who tried to kill him. Their conversation lasts for twenty minutes. Years on, the Pope will write in his book *Memory and Identity*: 'In the course of our conversation it became clear that Ali Ağca was still wondering how the attempted assassination could possibly have failed. He had planned it all meticulously, attending to every last detail... Ali Ağca had probably sensed that over and above his own power, over and above the power of shooting and killing, there was a higher power. He then began to look for it. I hope and pray that he found it.'

1999

The Pope asks the Italian president to drop the charges against Ali Ağca. Soon after, the terrorist leaves the Italian prison, but there is no question of his release. The Turks immediately arrest him and lock him up for the murder of Abdi İpekçi. He finds himself back in Kartal fortress prison.

8

Demirbağ lets me look through Ağca's dossier, where we find a letter he sent to the Pope. It is painstakingly written out, one letter at a time. Ağca has some paralysis in his right hand, so he writes by holding a pen in his clenched fist.

'He has kidney disease and bad lungs too,' adds Demirbağ.

At the sight of the letter the lawyer comes to life.

'The Pope was extremely important to Ağca. Now he is in prison because of a different matter, for the alleged murder of İpekçi.'

Alleged, because years on Ağca said he wasn't the one who shot İpekçi – he just kept watch in case someone came along.

'If he were an opportunist, he'd have forgotten about the Pope long ago,' Demirbağ continues. 'But he never stops talking about him! He recalls their meeting, and the fact that the Pope forgave him and embraced him like a son. Ağca loved him like a father too.

'When I started on Ağca's case I knew nothing about the Pope, the Vatican, or Christianity. But I soon realised that to understand my client I must understand the Polish Pope. Now I know he was a great man, the greatest that ever lived on this earth. Ali Ağca thinks so too. He wanted to go to his funeral – not to gain publicity, he simply wanted to be there. He wasn't able to go, but as soon as he is set free he will visit John Paul II's tomb. I know he misses him very much.'

9

Ağca and John Paul II only met once, in 1983, during the Pope's famous visit to the prison. Nevertheless, Ağca called him his greatest friend until the day he died. His brother insists that the friendship between Ali Ağca and John Paul II was so strong that if he wanted to, he could become a cardinal.

The Pope said that during their conversation Ağca was afraid of vengeance from Our Lady of Fatima, who – according to Catholics the world over – thwarted the assassination attempt. John Paul II reassured him. 'She loves you,' he says of Our Lady.

Ağca remembered that encounter differently.

'The Vatican wanted me to agree to be baptised – that was one of the reasons for the Pope's visit,' he told the Italian journalists. 'So we talked about religion. I told the Pope about the holy vision that came to me straight from God. The Pope believed me.'

To this day Ağca still claims to be the messiah.

He says he shot at the Pope because God told him to do it in person. 'At the last moment I wanted to give up, go to the Termini railway station, take the train back to Zurich and live in peace. And then a miracle happened. In a split second I realised I had to go back and shoot him,' he told the journalists.

Ağca says he was merely fulfilling a prophecy. He did it because someone had to. God wanted it to be Mehmet Ali Ağca, the new messiah, born into a poor family, in Hekimhan, near apricot-scented Malatya, in the frosty winter of 1958.

10

The Ağcas' flat is very modestly furnished. The main room is just two sofas, a television set, a faded old rug and the stove by which Fatma is sitting.

'Your brother says he is the messiah. What do you think about that?' I ask Ali's brother.

There's no reply. The uncles' heads are at a standstill, and the silence drags on relentlessly.

'We don't fully understand it,' Adnan finally answers. 'We're simple people, and that's a matter for the professors. But the prophecy of Fatima mentions my brother, doesn't it? And there it is written that the world has much suffering ahead of it. So far, it has all come true. When my brother comes out of prison he will write a book, in which he will explain everything. It will be like *The Da Vinci Code*, which showed the Christians what their religion is really like.'

Mustafa Demirbağ claims there's something in it too.

'At first I thought it was nonsense, but I changed my mind when Ağca was released. I saw how worn out he was, scared by what the papers were writing about him. "Killer set free!", "Satan is among us!" shouted the headlines. And there was Ağca, looking at me from above all this crap with the eyes of a child.'

'And what does that mean?'

'I realised that they were crucifying him. Just like Christ.'

2006

Ağca comes out of prison. The Turkish court counts the nineteen years he spent in jail in Italy as part of his sentence. On top of that, the judge acknowledges that Ağca came under an amnesty that was implemented several years ago.

However, the former terrorist is only free for eight days. He spends some of them with Adnan and Fatma, and the rest with Mustafa Demirbağ.

'We didn't do anything special,' says Adnan. 'Ali watched television, and we chatted a bit.'

'Once we went for a walk on the Bosporus, to the Kadıköy district,' says Demirbağ. 'Ağca put on a cap and dark glasses, in spite of which two people recognised him and asked for his autograph. I know it gave him pleasure. But what he enjoyed the most was not having to eat with a plastic knife and fork, and feeling the breeze blowing in his face. He told me: "You can't imagine how wonderful it feels to breathe the air as a free man".'

Where did Ağca stay? Demirbağ refuses to say. 'At the house of some friends,' he curtly replies.

Who sent a luxury limousine to the prison for him? The attorney says he doesn't know. 'The car was there, so we got in and drove off.'

The Turkish journalists write that it was the Grey Wolves who organised the car and the accommodation. They also write that it is his terrorist associates who pay for Ağca's lawyer and who have made sure he got out of prison as soon as possible. Nowadays many of them are businessmen, politicians, or highly placed people. They had no influence in the Italian jurisdiction, but apparently they do in the Turkish one.

Following Ağca's release from prison the Turkish press is outraged. It puts pressure on the minister of justice to order the court to re-examine the case, and a decision is made at record speed. Ağca has only been at liberty for eight days when the police come for him.

'I've been expecting you,' he says. The police officer who was in charge of the arrest will later say that Ağca put up no resistance. He wasn't surprised, maybe just a little sad.

Ağca goes back to Kartal fortress prison for another four years.

11

Nükhet İpekçi, daughter of Abdi, who was Ağca's first victim, will never forget the day her father was killed.

'It's not just my personal tragedy, it's a tragedy for the whole of Turkey. He was one of very few people who were able to put a stop to the terror,' she says.

On the day he died İpekçi was forty-nine years old. He blamed both the left and the right for the terrorism and anarchy. Neither the politicians nor the terrorists liked him, but they had to reckon with him, and that was why he was killed.

'The Pope made a big mistake by forgiving Ağca,' says İpekçi's daughter. 'You can forgive someone who asks you to. Ağca never asked. More than that, he never even apologised to my family for what happened. Did he apologise to the Pope? You see, he didn't do that either. He is coarse and insolent. If anyone asks him about the attack on my father, he's quite capable of laughing in their face. And then he keeps saying: "The Pope forgave me, you should do the same".'

Nükhet İpekçi wants the other former terrorists to be put behind bars as well. Oral Çelik, who coordinated the attack on her father as well as the one on the Pope, has never been in prison. He even wrote a book on the inside story of the attack on the Pope. He advertised it as 'the first 100-per-cent true' account.

'It's a load of rubbish,' is how one Turkish journalist describes Çelik's book. 'Its central idea is that it was the Vatican and the Italian secret service who provided the money for the assassination of the Pope. This is the theory that the Grey Wolves are now promoting vociferously, but no one in their right mind believes it's true.'

Until recently, Çelik was president of the Malatyaspor sports club – the one with the AstroTurf and the fans who sing about Ağca.

2010

Mehmet Ali Ağca was released in January 2010. He announced films and interviews giving 'the whole truth about the attack on the Pope', and even said he'd take part in the Turkish version of *Strictly Come Dancing*. His lawyer had assured me over the phone that Ağca would go and visit John Paul II's tomb in the Vatican, and that straight afterwards he would fly to Krakow and Wadowice (the Pope's birthplace).

At the same time he advised me that Ağca would never apologise to the İpekçi family, because there was nothing to apologise for.

However, when Ağca came out of prison, his lawyer stopped picking up the phone. A few days later the line went completely dead, since when I have not been able to get in touch with him.

I was still in touch with Adnan Ağca for quite a long time. We used to send each other text messages to wish each other all the best – I sent him one for Kurban Bayramı, and he sent me one for Christmas. He asked for help getting Polish citizenship for his entire family. He said that he didn't feel comfortable in Turkey. 'The Pope did say we were his family. Can members of the same family have different citizenships?' he asked.

But when his brother came out of prison, Adnan Ağca's phone fell silent too.

After his release, Mehmet Ali Ağca vanished into thin air.

bye bye bush

IT WAS LIKE THIS: dinner, briefing the troops, then talking to the officials. On 14th December 2008 George Bush said goodbye to Iraq. Finally he went out to face the journalists. He answered questions and bared his teeth in a grin. Just another official event.

Suddenly one of the journalists took off his shoe and hurled it at Bush.

'That's for you, you dog!' he shouted. 'From the widows and orphans of Iraq!' and quickly threw the other shoe.

Bush managed to duck. In their panic, his security agents trampled the White House spokeswoman – quite needlessly, as the attacker had run out of feet, and the Iraqi bodyguards had brought him to the ground.

the contractor from mosul

Later that day, a delivery van was bumping along a potholed road on the Turkish Black Sea coast. To stop himself from falling asleep, the Kurd driving it was chain-smoking cigarettes. He envied his boss, who was having a doze, resting his head against the window.

They were both brought back to life by the phone: +964...

an Iraqi number. Ramazan Baydan, thirty-something years old with three days' stubble, pressed the green receiver.

Six months later he tells me in broken Polish that he'd been waiting all his life for that call. He'd always had a feeling that one day someone would call and change his fate.

That someone was Abdullah, a contractor from Mosul.

'Ramazan! Have you seen the news?'

How could he have seen it? He'd spent all day delivering goods to shops along the coast.

'A guy threw his shoes at Bush in Baghdad ...'

'*Maşallah*! That's great! Did he hit him?'

'No.'

'Then why are you bothering me?'

'Ramazan! It's the only thing they're talking about on television today. The papers are going to be full of it too!'

'So what?'

'Ramazan! They were YOUR shoes!'

the sole hurts the most

Imam Halil Yusuf has a problem with the shoe thrown at Bush. He examines it from the left side, then the right. He puts it on the floor, and then picks it up again.

'I bought them on impulse. They're from the same factory. Look, they've even called them... Help me, it's in English... "Bye Bye Bush". It's a Bye Bye Bush! If I'd been in that guy's place, I'd have thrown it too.'

We're sitting down at the imam's house, right next to the mosque on the Asian side of Istanbul, having a cup of tea. The imam, who is close to sixty with a grey beard and two deep wrinkles on his forehead, is thinking aloud.

'I'd have thrown it. But I'm ashamed of the fact. Islam is a religion of love. If somebody wrongs you, you must turn the other cheek. On the other hand, Bush is a murderer and one can only praise the Iraqi. He aimed so the sole would hit him.' We both look at the thick sole of the Bye Bye Bush. 'Here it's a major insult,' says the imam, but he finds it impossible to hide his sympathy for the shoe-thrower. 'Except that this isn't about a shoe. It's not even about Bush,' he adds, combing his beard with his fingers. 'It's about you people. Here there are more and more angry feelings towards the West – towards America, the EU, towards you. I run a centre for drug addicts. For years I've been going to conferences all over Europe. I always say that although we have different ways of life, our problems are the same – how to give our children a better future, how to guarantee old people a dignified death, and how to make the world a peaceful place.

'But for you people living in peace means living according to your rules. You say Islam is backward, our democracy is weak, and our traditions are foolish. You tell us to change, because it's you people who know how one should live in the twenty-first century. And when we try to change – and in fact we've been doing nothing else ever since Atatürk's day – you laugh at us. I for instance have a beard and a Muslim cap. If I go out into the city, you take photos of me! Like some sort of monkey!'

'But *hodja*, that's just curiosity, not mockery,' I try to soothe him.

'No, Witold, it's more than that. My country wants to be Western and modern at any price. We'd do anything to be liked by you. Half a century ago we sent troops to Korea so the Americans would take notice of us. And what did we get in return? Nothing! They didn't even lift our visa restrictions. We dress in jeans, we make films that imitate yours. But you keep on coming here and turning up your noses.'

'Not everyone does...'

'Witold, it's hard talking to you. Instead of upsetting me, why don't you go and ask the people who buy those... Bye Bye Bushes?'

iraq is proud

The footwear attack was carried out by a journalist called Muntadhar al-Zaidi. A childless bachelor, he is twenty-nine years old.

'This sort of president gets that sort of attack,' said a Turkish satirist the day after.

'I think he couldn't bear that bastard's grin,' Dhirgham al-Zaidi, the attacker's brother, tells me over the phone. 'It was his third year working for al-Baghdadia television. At the start I was his cameraman. Every day we showed what life was like for the poorest Iraqis, the widows, orphans and cripples. The war did terrible things here. You don't see it on your televisions. You have censorship, because it's your war and your fault. Apart from that, your journalists are afraid to venture there. Muntadhar wasn't afraid. He was strongly affected by what he saw. Our dearest cousin was killed in an attack. Every family has lost someone. Throw a shoe? I never expected him to do that. I think he acted on impulse. But I'm very proud of him.'

Almost all Iraqis were proud. When it turned out that al-Zaidi was in danger of spending some fifteen years in prison, thousands of them came out onto the streets to express their solidarity with 'Hurling Muntadhar'. They were carrying shoes – in their hands and tied to sticks – and set about gluing them to pictures of Bush's face while shouting: 'American dog!'

As soon as he had calmed down following the call from Baghdad, Ramazan Baydan went straight to the nearest hotel. His shoe was being shown on every single news bulletin; the hotel television set received Turkish and Georgian channels, and also Iranian ones, though with a snowy picture.

'I wept,' Baydan tells me six months later. 'I designed that shoe myself, and for the first five years I stuck them together myself too, because I have to see to everything in person. And now the whole world was admiring my shoe!

'However, I knew I had to act quickly. Only a day later ten other factories started boasting that it was their shoes that had been thrown at Bush – two from China, one from Syria and one each from Lebanon and Iraq. The rest were from Turkey, because we produce most of the clothing in the region. I saw an idiot on Iraqi television who was waving a sandal about, saying it was his shoe that was thrown by Hurling Munthadar. I'd have torn him to pieces with my bare hands! Anyone can see the Bye Bye Bush flies slowly, which is the only reason why Bush had the chance to duck. It was a heavy shoe, not a flimsy wedding slipper.'

our banks are better than your banks

Recep, the owner of a small cake shop, is quite sure the Bye Bye Bush is not a flimsy slipper.

'I put them on for my cousin's circumcision and my feet were too hot all day. It was unbearable. Maybe that fellow from Iraq couldn't bear to wear them in that heat either? He took them off, but had nowhere to put them, so he threw them at Bush,' jokes the cake-maker, and boasts that he has already had several orders for cakes in the shape of a shoe. 'Ever since it turned out to be a Turkish shoe, everyone's talking about it! I agree that Turkish means better. Turkish and Arabic, in other words, Islamic. Did you know that our banks haven't felt the effects of the crisis at all? Well, the Turkish banks have felt it a bit, the ones that idolise your West. But the Islamic ones, run on the principles of the Quran, are doing better and better.'

And Recep tells me about the bank that lent him money to get his business going.

'The Quran forbids earning interest, and rightly so. It's always a poor man who borrows from a rich one, and he always loses on it. The rich man gets even richer, but the poor man never gets out of debt to the day he dies.

'Look how your banks work. They only give you money if they get a guarantee that you'll pay it back. If your business doesn't work out, you have to sell your house. Or one of your kidneys.

'An Islamic bank offered me a partnership according to Islamic principles. If the cake shop doesn't do well, both I and the bank will lose. No one will drag me through the courts or send retribution. We have a joint interest in it being a success. The bank gives me money and advice, and we write a business plan together. We also earn money together.

'If all banks operated like that, there wouldn't be a crisis. But your entire culture is based on money. The Muslim always remembers his family and friends. He always shares with poorer people. You lot want to have as much as possible for yourselves. If he has somewhere to live and something to eat, a Muslim thanks Allah and regards it as great good fortune. You people in the West need a car as well. And a helicopter. And the latest phone.

'That's how I think, but the young people are completely different. My son is thirty years old and he's got a stud in his chin. He listens to horrible music and he thinks, the fool, that he is a European.'

shoes like pistachios

The World Centre for Plotting Against Bush – as one of the Turkish commentators called Baydan's factory – is located on the outskirts of Istanbul.

From the city centre it takes almost an hour to get there by suburban railway. Or two hours by taxi – the traffic jams in this city of fifteen million only come to an end on the outskirts of Küçükçekmece, a village which was recently swallowed up by the vast spread of Istanbul. This is where the Janissary units used to stop for a rest when they set off to conquer Europe. The troops of Kara Mustafa also stopped in Küçükçekmece on their way to Vienna. To this day, life moves slowly here, far from any major global conflict.

Veiled by a headscarf, the secretary offers coffee, tea or Cola Turka, the local answer to Coca-Cola, which is often advertised on TV by Hollywood actors.

Soon after, the boss himself appears.

'I am big-boss Ramazan,' he introduces himself. That is all he can say in English. He gets on much better, though imperfectly, in Polish. 'Good shoes, very cheaply,' he says, pointing at the products displayed on the shelves. 'I was spend three years going to Warsaw, to stadium,' he says, twisting his tongue, so he switches to Turkish and tells me that before flying in the direction of George W. Bush, model number 271 led a nomadic life with the big-boss, travelling to the bazaar that used to operate on the site of Warsaw's 10th-Anniversary Stadium and the street markets in Polish towns including Mława, Grodzisk and Piaseczno.

'I didn't make much money in Poland, but the people were great. They achieved everything on their own, just like me. There were a lot of Kurds, like at home. Apart from that there were Turks, Bulgarians, Russians and Ukrainians. It was only in 2003, when the war erupted in Iraq, that I stopped going to your country.

'Iraq was the business opportunity of a lifetime. Everyone was afraid to sell there, but I used to go to the small towns, sometimes a week after the front had gone through, and I'd look for a sales outlet. I'd think to myself, war is war, but people have still got to walk about in something. And I was right.

'Other people are only discovering this market now, but I've already got contacts. I sell shoes in Turkey, Iraq, Syria, Jordan, Russia, Albania, Bosnia... I'll give you the addresses of a few shops at the bazaar, and you'll see for yourselves. My shoes sell as quickly as Iranian pistachios!'

So we go and have a chat with the buyers. The first shop has already run out of Bye Bye Bushes.

'We sell two hundred pairs a week,' boasts the owner's son.

In the second shop the salesman starts with an anti-Bush tirade 'I hope he has nightmares. I hope he can't sleep and will suffer dreadfully to the day he dies. For the number of people he's killed in Iraq, his place is in hell, between Hitler and Stalin. So you're from Poland? Meaning your hands are red with blood too. I hope your children will be ashamed of this war.'

We give up, and go into a third shop, in the very middle of the Aksaray district. In the communist era this is where the Polish dealers used to get their supplies of leather and jeans. Apparently there's still a shop somewhere round here with the Polish name Boniek, but nowadays it's the Russians who rule the roost.

'Bye Bye Bushes? Yes indeed! Tan, black or brown. All with the brand label and a short farewell message for the former president,' says the salesman, touting his wares. 'You want to talk to the customers? Be my guest! Oh, this is a customer we've befriended. Mehmet! Come and say something to the newspaper!'

your king tied our bootlaces

'In Turkish the United States are called the ABD, *Amerika Birleşik Devletleri*,' says Mehmet, and everyone else in the shop listens to him closely. Mehmet sells the sesame-coated bread rings known here as *simit* on the street. But he finished high school, and apparently even went to college for a year. He is held in high regard by the local tradesmen.

Mehmet has no doubt that these days the ABD is the most important player on the global chessboard.

'But once upon a time we were the ABD. We ruled the whole

world, from Belgrade to Mecca. Did you know, Witold, that we got all the way to Vienna?'

For a few seconds I wonder whether to carry on with this theme, which must surely be painful for Turkish pride. You only die once.

'I know. Our king chased you out of there.'

Mehmet looks at me as if I'm one of the lunatics who sometimes hang around outside mosques.

'Are you off your head, Witold? Your king? The Polack king? He was only fit to tie the bootlaces of the Turkish Janissaries.' Mehmet whoops with laughter, and so do the salesmen and customers, who are forming an ever bigger circle by the minute.

This time my pride is hurt.

'But he routed you at the battle of Vienna!'

Mehmet throws up his hands

'We routed ourselves. One pasha quarrelled with another. There was a lot of in-fighting among the cliques at court. The sultan didn't suppress it, and we came apart. Whatever the case may be, we sure do know how to quarrel. But when we were the ABD, everybody had an equal chance. A slave could become the sultan. It was known to happen. No matter if he was a Bosniak, a Circassian or a Kurd. Now anyone who is born poor, dies poor. And they call it democracy.'

our sheep is very well

Once Mehmet has left, one of the female customers comes up to me discreetly.

'Are you from a newspaper? Did you know that our scientists cloned a sheep?' she asks softly.

Well I never! And I thought it was the British.

'They were the first,' agrees the customer, who turns out to be a biology teacher. 'But their Dolly died after a year. Our Oyalı is two years old now, and is still doing pretty well. To me that's typical of your West – poor quality. You'll wear a pair of Bye Bye Bushes for ten years or more. But I bought these shoes from Italy and they fell apart after a week – look here.' And the biology teacher shows me how her shoe is coming apart at the seams.

'From Italy? If you please, madam, my cousin makes those shoes just outside Istanbul,' pipes up the salesman.

The biology teacher snorts at him and at me, and goes off with her nose in the air.

the bye bye bush as a symbol of the struggle

Let's be frank – Ramazan Baydan's shoes are total rubbish. I don't believe they would last any longer than the biology teacher's Italian shoes from just outside Istanbul. They're made of poor imitation leather. The soles are so thick that any man taller than a garden gnome looks as if he wants to give himself more height by wearing them. Now they're made even more ugly by the label – on a golden-yellow background, sure enough, it says: 'Bye Bye Bush'.

But like any Turkish businessman, Baydan is a master of turning defects into virtues.

'It's a cheap shoe. It only costs thirty dollars. Thanks to that it can symbolise the struggle of the poor against the rich,' he says, glancing at the notes he has hidden in a drawer. 'My shoe has become the symbol of the struggle!' he reads. 'My company will be supporting dialogue in the Middle East. I'll be helping the Palestinians, the Chechens and the Gaza Strip. The Bye Bye Bush will be a weapon in the fight for world peace.'

How exactly his company, Baydan Ayakkabı, is going to exert an influence on the world leaders is a fact its boss does not betray. Seeing that his predictions have not made much of an impression on me, he shuts the drawer and offers me a cigarette.

pamuk vilifies the nation

'Peace in the Middle East? Not in our lifetime,' says Zeynep, a student from Istanbul. 'I'm buying this pair for my father. He was an officer. He has just retired. He too thinks the Israelis and the Arabs will never come to terms.'

'Why does he need the shoes? Well, there are a number of people you might want to throw them at in Turkey too,' says Zeynep, weighing up a Bye Bye Bush in the palm of her hand. 'Several politicians. Singers. And that bloody Orhan Pamuk.'

Politicians – that's obvious. They're always up to no good. Singers? They're often out of tune. But what harm has the Nobel prize-winning writer done to the student? We leave the shop and go for a cup of coffee. I ask Zeynep for a short lecture on the point where literature meets life.

'First of all, he has never done a single day's work in his life. He's from a rich family. But there are writers who have to starve themselves in order to write. Why doesn't anyone give them the Nobel prize?'

I reply that if they only gave it to poor people, it would be aid, not the Nobel prize. Zeynep shakes her head.

'Do you know why Pamuk got the Nobel prize? Because he vilifies the Turkish nation! He laughs at us for being proud of our history, and for continuing to commemorate our army's greatest victories. Or for being unable to find a place for ourselves between East and West. Writers should reinforce everything that's fine about their nation, but he laughs at everything that's petty about us. But what hurts me most of all is that he maligns Atatürk.'

And Zeynep reminds me how after the First World War the neighbouring countries wanted to carve Turkey up, but Atatürk wouldn't let them. And how he reformed and brought her country closer to Europe.

'Turkey cannot change any of his message!' says the officer's daughter excitedly. 'If somebody maligns him, it's like an electric current going through me. Only five years ago Atatürk was sacred, but now Pamuk, who mocks him, gets the Nobel prize. And some pseudo-film director makes a film in which Atatürk gets drunk and behaves badly.* I don't care if he really did get drunk or not! I don't want to know that side of him! But wait a minute, here comes my friend. He's really smart, he's sure to tell you something interesting. Muraaat!'

Murat is at college with Zeynep, studying education.

'The West? I come into contact with it almost every day. My home town of Alanya is on the coast. There are thousands of tourists there. When I see how you treat women, it makes my blood boil,' he tells me. 'Your woman talks to any man. Someone accosts her, and she smiles!'

'They're in a foreign country. They're just trying to be nice.'

'Only prostitutes make eyes at everyone. But what sort of husbands are you? Whenever they meet someone from the West, my friends always have a joke with them. Where are you from, Poland? I once slept with a Polish girl... Well, why don't you say something?'

'What am I supposed to say? You lucky guy...'

'But man, I've just insulted you!'

'Have you?'

'That's just it – you people don't understand a thing. For a remark like that a Turk would instantly hit you in the face. It's as if I'd insulted your family,' says Murat, and walks away.

'Lots of boys think like that, especially in the villages,' says Zeynep. 'It's like tribal relations. Anyone from your tribe is your kin. When it comes to how women are treated,' says Zeynep, pausing to think for quite a while, 'then actually I side with the West.'

---

* Can Dündar's film is called *Mustafa* and it shows Atatürk privately, which stirred enormous controversy in Turkey.

one president throws his shoe at another

A month after Munthadar's exploit, the Indian minister of internal affairs had a shoe thrown at him by a journalist. The next one flew in the direction of the Chinese prime minister during a visit to Oxford. Then the president of Brazil threatened the president of Venezuela with his shoe. 'I'll throw it if you go over the time for your statement,' he said during a South American summit meeting.

In the Iraqi city of Tikrit a local artist put up a monument to the Bye Bye Bush, and in the USA some youthful opponents of President Bush took to wearing badges featuring a shoe.

Ramazan Baydan began to shave and wear scent. He also had a marriage proposal (from a rich lady in the US who doesn't like Bush either), and the offer of an affair (from a model who used to advertise his shoes). He rejected both. Nowadays he has no time for anything except the company.

The company meanwhile is under siege. Before the famous incident, model number 271 had sold about 5,000 pairs a year. But since becoming the Bye Bye Bush, in only six months more than 30,000 have gone, most of them to... the United States.

'People who don't like Bush put them on top of their TV sets,' says Baydan. 'I'm just worried that sales growth has been poor in Iraq. They don't believe it was my shoe. If I can convince them, I might get one-third of the Iraqi shoe market. Just like Saddam's tailor, who tops the market for suits there since his trial.'

'Who's that?'

'He's called Recep Cesur. I'll give you his address.'

saddam hussein had excellent taste

Jacket size – 56
Leg – 112
Height – 1.86m
Shoe size – 45

Kurdish tailor Recep Cesur, bald as a billiard ball, quotes all these numbers by heart.

'Not because they relate to Saddam,' he stresses. 'I remember the size of every regular customer.'

His shop in the famous bazaar in the Sultanahmet district has been under siege for several years. Inside there's no chance of a quiet chat, so we go behind the scenes. Cesur shows me a curio: Saddam Hussein's final suit, which was never collected.

'Before the trial his cousin ordered eight suits and shirts from me. I didn't know if they were for Saddam. His entire family has its clothes made here, and they gave a different jacket size from the usual one. But when I saw how haggard he'd become, it all made sense. He was eager to look good at the trial, so he put on my suits, nothing else. There was just this last one that I wasn't in time to send him.'

Cesur had been tailoring for Saddam, his ministers, and even the Iraqi football team for decades, but it was the former Iraqi president's trial that marked the start of his years of plenty.

'Every time Saddam reached for his pen, the camera showed my firm's logo stitched into his suit,' boasts the tailor. 'One journalist reckoned I'd have had to pay six million dollars for that sort of advertising. Before then we'd been selling twelve thousand suits a year, but after the trial that figure increased fivefold, mainly in the Middle East.'

'Isn't it a paradox that the suits of Saddam Hussein, who was sentenced to death for killing Kurds, were made by another Kurd?' I ask.

'Saddam didn't know who made them. And for me business is business, and it shouldn't be mixed with politics.'

the eu wants to crush turkey

I go back to the shop selling Bye Bye Bushes. A stylish man is trying on some sand-coloured shoes. In fluent English he invites me for coffee, and at once starts tugging off his tie.

'In a tie I'm a civil servant for one of the Istanbul local authorities. Don't write which one. When I take it off, I'm an ordinary citizen called Murat. I want to answer your questions as a citizen,' he says, draping the blue tie over his chair. 'Bush and the shoe? It's a really good thing it happened. That guy did what we'd all like to do. It's a pity he missed. I bought some of those shoes, and I'm looking forward to some EU officials coming to visit us. Why? Because you're aiming to deprive Turkey of its national identity.'

I've almost choked on my coffee.

'Sorry?'

'Of course you are! You know what a strong country we are, and that in a few years we'll be able to give the whole of Europe a good thrashing. So you come along and promote condoms, gay marriage and sex without obligations – everything to make us have fewer children.'

'Or maybe to avoid having hungry, unwanted children? And so everyone can live as they wish?

'You're trying to fool me, like everyone from the West. No child goes hungry in Turkey. Islam tells us to look after the poor. And we do. But the EU is promoting deviant behaviour. Whenever there's a parade of deviants in Istanbul they carry an EU flag. There must be some reason for that. Our prime minister says: "Let's join – they'll give us lots of money". But at what cost? A delegation came to our office, including a Frenchwoman, a Belgian and a man from

Luxembourg. And at once they started mouthing away: "You've got terrible bureaucracy and there's sure to be corruption here. We're going to fight against the corruption."

'The boss kept them waiting in the corridor all week. He said he hadn't time for a meeting, and they had to leave before he could receive them. He showed them who's in charge here. Our bureaucracy has five hundred years of tradition – continuity since Ottoman times. And the EU isn't going to teach us what to do!

'Once upon a time, I admit, I used to be full of admiration for the West. But when I spent a year living in Hamburg I found out there's nowhere as beautiful or as rich as in Turkey. You're jealous of us – that's why you want us to join the Union. And then you'll be in charge here.'

'Is there anything about the West that you like?'

Murat thinks hard.

'I liked Obama, to begin with. But that's in the past now, because he came to Istanbul and said: "The EU must take in Turkey!" Hello hello! This isn't his country and it's none of his business! He could say he likes our ancient monuments, or our cuisine. But whether and what we should join is something we shall decide for ourselves. Not long ago there was a poll on the matter. These days more than sixty per cent of Turks don't want your Union at all.'

the next crisis will kill you

Halil and Rabia are anti-Union too.

'I think we'd lose more than we'd gain,' says Halil. They live in Konya. He has a trimmed Muslim beard, and she is in a headscarf. They've come to do some shopping; Halil's father runs a clothes shop. 'Your time is coming to an end!' adds Halil, and Rabia modestly drops her gaze. 'Bush's era is already over. Yours is ending too, Witold. That goes for all of you people.'

They've been married for six months. They've never been to the West and they're not curious about it, but Halil has been on a pilgrimage to Syria.

'To begin with, when I saw the shoe attack, I was furious. You send tanks, bombers and crack troops against us Muslims. And in reply we try to smack you with a shoe. Even Bush laughed at that.

'But one wise mullah explained to me: "The West will destroy itself". In ten years' time nobody will remember that you were ever a power. One – because you don't want to have children. Two – because you've got it too good. As the proverb says, a well-fed lion forgets how to hunt. You may yet survive this crisis, but you won't survive the next one. And three – because you eat pork. You may laugh, but Mohammed knew what he was doing when he forbade us to. Pigs are dirty. They spread diseases. Any new swine flu epidemic could be your last.'

'The boy may be right about the pigs,' says imam Halil Yusuf when I summarise my conversations for him. 'And the collapse of your civilisation... Maybe there's something in it... The Muslims definitely don't like the fact that you people are always right. Your culture, your democracy, your ideas are the best. In a country with such rich traditions as ours that can't possibly go down well. In Poland there were still monkeys jumping about in the trees when there was civilisation on the Tigris and the Euphrates. Both those rivers flow through Turkey. You should respect that.'

'*Hodja*, there were never any monkeys in Poland...'

'Witold, you're annoying me. You'd better go now.'

a turkish mixture

According to sociologist Dr Hatice Öztürk, 'the Turkish man is made up of a bizarre mixture of pride in the past and modern-day complexes. We are all proud of what a powerful country we once were,' she explains. 'Nowadays there are far fewer reasons to be proud. Indeed, we won the Eurovision Song Contest, and we're not bad at football. But the days when the sultan's army ventured all the way to Vienna will never come back again.

'However, you need to be aware that only a particular kind of person buys Bye Bye Bushes. That's why you came upon so many religious types, and that's why they were so sharply critical of the West. Hundreds of thousands of people in Turkey live quite successfully "in Western style". I think of myself as that sort of person, though I admit that if you said something nasty about Turkish cuisine or Atatürk, I'd be deeply offended.'

obama and the apricots

Three months after George Bush's visit to Iraq, Barack Obama came to Istanbul. An hour after his plane left, the phone rang in the Malatya city mayor's office.

'Ahmet, did you see the news?'

'No, what is it?'

'Obama ate an apricot. He nicked one for himself at the bazaar.'

'And what of it?'

'Ahmet, for the love of Allah, it was one of YOUR apricots!'

Malatya is the world's biggest producer of apricots. That very same day a special committee was set up at the mayor's office. Two days later some students presented their designs for a poster. A week later a picture of Obama appeared in the papers, surrounded by apricots from Malatya. 'He knows what's good', announced the hastily cooked-up slogan.

'On the one hand you hate us. On the other, your approval is invaluable to us,' says Dr Öztürk, smiling.

nazım

TURKEY'S GREATEST POET had the Polish surname Borzęcki and used to stay as a guest at the Polish parliament building.

Even though he couldn't understand a word of Turkish, the great Polish poet Julian Tuwim would listen to his poems as if spellbound. Poet and soldier Władysław Broniewski used to take him out drinking. And a woman called Halina from just outside Ostrołęka wrote him a letter to say she wanted to live with him and have his babies.

It's not surprising. Nazım Hikmet Borzęcki was a living legend. He had spent more than ten years in prison in defence of communism. Crowds of people came to his public readings, and every new volume of poetry he published was a major event.

The Turkish poet was always emphasising that the Poles are hospitable people, and the Polish landscape is beautiful, yet he also admitted that it was hard for him to live away from Istanbul. He felt homesick, but he had burned all his bridges.

atatürk

1

To tell the story of this great poet, we have to go a short way back in time, initially to the First World War, in which the crumbling

Ottoman Empire took part on the German side.

'The sultan is losing the war. Our neighbours and the Great Powers are carving up our country like cooks slicing a kebab skewered on a spit,' says Süleyman Akçay, a historian from Istanbul. 'The terrified ruler signs an act of capitulation. He hands over the Aegean Sea coast to the Greeks, and allows the east to be divided up by the Entente powers, the Armenians and the Kurds.'

Akçay tells the story with as much involvement as if he had taken part in these crucial events himself. He gesticulates, deepens his voice, and makes dramatic pauses. It's hard to believe he is talking about historical events that happened almost a hundred years ago.

That's how the Turks behave whenever the conversation involves Atatürk.

'The young officers refuse to let the country be divided. Under the leadership of the charismatic Mustafa Kemal they take up the fight,' says Akçay. 'Thanks to his genius they win the war against Greece and take power away from the sultan. Mustafa Kemal becomes the first president.'

Thus begins a story which every Turkish child can recite, even if woken in the middle of the night. As president, Kemal sets the bar extremely high for himself. In the course of a decade he aims to change a benighted leviathan into a modern country, and the traditional fez-wearing Turk into a New Turk – a rightful citizen of Europe. To this day the great sweep of this project has been an inspiration for many world leaders (including the former Shah of Iran Mohammad Reza Pahlavi, the first president of Tunisia Habib Bourguiba, the former president of Pakistan Pervez Musharraf, and lately the Georgian president Mikheil Saakashvili).

'He carries out reforms like no one else on earth,' says Akçay. 'Instead of the Islamic calendar he introduces the European one. Instead of sharia law, a modern penal code. Instead of government by the clergy, secularism. He gives women voting rights far earlier than a number of countries in Europe. He changes the alphabet from Arabic to Latin. Surnames are to be more Turkish. He changes his own name too, and from 1934 he is called Atatürk – the Father of the Turks.'

2

Atatürk's reforms turned Turkish life on its head the length and breadth of the country.

'They weren't really reforms,' says one of my Turkish friends. 'It was more like creating the country from scratch. Until then we had been the centre of the Islamic world. We used to take care of Mecca and Medina. And suddenly we became a country at war against religion.'

Whence the change? In the 1920s and 1930s the entire world was asking this question, so the Turkish government dispatched envoys to explain to foreign diplomats what the reforms were all about. 'The unity of Islam is a myth which can only gain a new lease of life from a reborn Turkish nation,' said the Turkish envoy at the Polish diplomatic mission in Berlin. 'We shall no longer be regarded as a land of muezzins and harems. As a result, the artificial wall which has separated the Turks from modern life is coming down.'*

His words were confirmed by Atatürk's actions. He did not hesitate to send out the troops, and ordered them to shoot men who refused to remove their fezzes. 'Civilised, international attire is right and proper for our nation, and we shall wear it. Shoes on our feet, trousers, shirts and ties, jackets and waistcoats – and naturally, to complete the set, headgear with

---

* This and the two following quotations are from a pamphlet by Professor Marcin Kula entitled *Pod górkę do Europy. O Turcji lat trzydziestych – ale też trochę o dzisiejszej Polsce* ('Up the hill to Europe: on Turkey in the 1930s, but also partly on today's Poland'), Warsaw, 1994.

a brim. I would like that to be clear. This form of headgear is called a hat,' said the Father of the Turks, as he introduced the so-called Hat Law of 1925.

On another occasion he criticised the Muslim *charshaf* (veil): 'I have seen women wearing a piece of material on their heads, a towel or something of the kind, to cover their faces... What is the point and the meaning of such behaviour? Can mothers and daughters really accept such strange habits, such a barbaric attitude? It is a spectacle that makes the entire nation the object of ridicule.'

Süleyman Akçay, the historian from Istanbul, has great respect for these words: 'What courage he had! Even his own mother wore the veil! But she did not live to see those reforms.'

celaleddin

1

To tell the story of the poet who used to stay at the Polish parliament building, we must go back even further in time. It is the year 1876. The brave general Mustafa Celaleddin is shot while fighting against the Montenegrins. He is hit in the stomach, and dies.

The Ottoman warriors grieved for their courageous commander – the sort who went out against the enemy in the front ranks, armed with nothing but a sabre.

Three horses were killed under him, and he was wounded six times. The first time it happened, he was not yet a Muslim and did not have a long beard or a turban. That was in his former life; Celaleddin used to be called Konstanty Borzęcki, and he was once a clerical student at a seminary in the Polish town of Włocławek.

He came from an impoverished gentry family, and wanted to become a painter. He had talent, and studied for two years at Warsaw's School of Fine Arts. But his family couldn't afford such fancies, so Konstanty had to give up painting and train to be a priest.

However, in 1848 the young Borzęcki ran away from the seminary and joined the Greater Poland Uprising. When the uprising failed, he went abroad – with the help of the Paris-based Hôtel Lambert group of Polish political exiles – to Turkey, without telling his relatives. In his biography of Borzęcki, *Pasza z Lechistanu* ('The Pasha from Lechistan'), historian of the Orient Jerzy S. Łątka suspects that his aristocratic family bore a grudge against him for having left the seminary.

In Turkey, like thousands of other Poles, the former insurgent converted to Islam and began a career in the Ottoman army.

2

Borzęcki was an excellent soldier, but he also made a name for himself as a writer. Once he was living abroad he posed himself the question: is Turkey in Europe or Asia? And he gave the answer in his book *Les Turcs anciens et modernes*.

Bernard Lewis, a leading expert on Turkey and its endless transformation into a modern state, mentions this book as one of the harbingers of Atatürk's reforms. Half a century before the Father of the Turks, Borzęcki proved that the Turks are just as much a European nation as the French or the Poles. He called his concept 'Turco-Arianism', and he promoted the idea of changing the alphabet from Arabic to Latin.

Fifty years later Atatürk would underline several hundred passages in Borzęcki's book. Beside the chapter about language he would write: 'To be done!'

And he did it – changing the alphabet was one of his major reforms.

Jerzy S. Łątka calls Borzęcki the Forefather of the Turks.

'That Pole deserves a statue of pure gold,' Atatürk himself said of Celaleddin-Borzęcki.

hikmet

1

Fifty years after the death of Celaleddin, the Father of the Turks ends the war with Greece and starts his reforms. At the same time a group of ragamuffins make their way from Istanbul to Ankara, the new capital. They are young poets. Among them is the most talented of all, Nazım Hikmet. His father was a general, his grandfather was the last Turkish governor of Salonica, the city where Atatürk was born, and his great-grandfather was Mustafa Celaleddin-Borzęcki.

Hikmet and his friends want to offer their skills in support of the new government. Atatürk likes their enthusiasm.

'He urged them to write poems "for a reason", not just for the sake of writing,' says Rabia Çiçek, who is writing her thesis on Hikmet's pre-war years. 'Meaning, to support his reforms.'

Hikmet is delighted by Atatürk. But soon after, proletarian fervour takes hold in Russia. The poet goes to study in Moscow. He admires Meyerhold's plays, makes friends with Mayakovsky, and falls in love with Lenin's ideas.

According to Rabia Çiçek: 'Years later he recalled that it was the march from Istanbul to Ankara that made him into a communist. That was when the young, pampered boy from a rich family first came into contact with poverty, the first time he ever saw people who had no money for food. The idea began to germinate in him that it was for those people that the world should be changed. He came back from Moscow as a 100-per-cent communist, to start a proletarian revolution on the Bosporus.'

2

In the 1930s the Turkish government is becoming increasingly authoritarian. Relations with the USSR are not yet on a knife edge, but the Soviet comrades have plans for expansion, among others in Turkey's direction, which cannot be popular on the Bosporus.

As a genuine, militant communist, now and then Hikmet ends up in prison for his views. However, Atatürk remembers that he is the great-grandson of Celaleddin-Borzęcki, and each time the poet is soon released. He gains fame from his letters-in-verse, narrated by a young Ethiopian who addresses them to his wife, Taranta Babu.

> Life is a beautiful thing,
> Taranta Babu!
> It's a beautiful, beautiful thing
> To understand like a wise tome
> to sense like a love song
> to wonder at like a child and to live
> to live, to live!

'He too loved life so much that he was ready to die for it,' a good friend of his will tell me many years later.

3

For Turkish poetry, Hikmet is like the classic Polish poets Mikołaj Rej, Jan Kochanowski and Adam Mickiewicz rolled into one. This comparison was thought up by his friend and translator, Małgorzata Łabęcka-Koecherowa.

He is Rej, because just as Rej was in Polish, Hikmet is one of the first to write poetry in the Turkish vernacular. Until then, incomprehensible, overblown Divan poetry had been produced in the Ottoman world. Turkish was regarded as the language of the peasantry, and was not held in high esteem.

He is Kochanowski because he brought Turkish to perfection. Interestingly, Hikmet learned to read and write when they were still using the Arabic alphabet, but wrote his poetry in the Latin one.

He is Mickiewicz because he appealed to ordinary people, on top of which there is a lot of the spirit of Romanticism in him.

According to Turkologist Professor Tadeusz Majda: 'He has an incredible feel for words. His poems can't possibly be translated, because he is excellent at setting one word beside another, and at playing with their ambiguities and phonetic similarities.'

the doctor

1

The Father of the Turks dies in 1938. A few months later Hikmet is accused of inciting soldiers to mutiny. The proof? A volume of his poetry is found under the bed of an army cadet. The sentence? Twenty-eight years in prison.

2

While Hikmet is in jail, the juggernaut of the Second World War rolls across the world. As soon as the post-war dust settles, Europe is cast into the shadow of the Iron Curtain.

The atmosphere of those years is superbly expressed by the following joke:

'Daddy, is there going to be a Third World War?'

'No, son, but we're going to fight for peace to the last drop of our blood.'

With this principle in mind, Stalin convokes the Soviet Committee for the Defence of Peace, malevolently known as Mr Stalin's Circus. This committee remembers the imprisoned Turkish communist, and appeals to Turkey to release him. Various left-wing artists and literary figures fight for his liberty, including Picasso, Neruda and Sartre, and they are joined by thousands of people the world over.

In the Second World War, Turkey remained neutral. In the Cold War, however, it declares itself to be on the side of the West. It is one of only two NATO members who share a border with the USSR, which is a source of extreme tension. For years on end the Russians try to destabilise the situation in Turkey. They finance left-wing extremists, the Communist Party, and also the Kurds, who are fighting for independence. Nothing associated with Moscow is well-regarded in Turkey, least of all communism.

However, in 1950, twelve years after Hikmet's imprisonment, the Turks soften their attitude, and Hikmet is released, but a few months later he is called up to join the army. He is to serve in the east of the country, where the temperature can rise above 40°C.

For years the poet has suffered from heart disease. Any physical strain is dangerous for him.

'I must record that you are fit, but your heart will not cope with military service,' the doctor tells him.

refık

Hikmet has no alternative. He has to escape.

His close friend Refık Erduran borrows a small motorboat from an acquaintance. He plans to use it to take the poet to Bulgaria and request asylum for him there.

I meet Refık at a café in Istanbul. He is just over eighty, but with a physique younger men might envy.

'Nazım was afraid I didn't know how to drive the boat,' he says. 'But I had done my homework. My cousin was a commander in the Turkish fleet, so I told him I was checking the script for a film about smugglers sailing between Turkey and Bulgaria. He gave everything away – where the patrols were, how to avoid them and how not to get ourselves shot by the Bulgarian border guards.'

Nevertheless Nazım is afraid to go. Ten years later, in his poem *Autobiography* he writes: 'In '51 I sailed with a young friend into the teeth of death.'*

---

* *Poems of Nazım Hikmet*, translated by Randy Blasing and Mutlu Konuk, New York, 2002.

'That's poetic licence,' says Refik, laughing. 'It was a beautiful day in July. Not a cloud in the sky.'

The gentlemen while away the time smoking cigarettes. Suddenly they see a small dot on the horizon, which turns out to be a Romanian ship.

According to Erduran: 'Nazım started shouting that his name was Hikmet and he wanted asylum. They responded with insults, because they'd had to stop that whole great big ship because of us. It was a while before they realised what it was all about.'

But instead of duly welcoming the great communist, the captain shuts him in isolation.

'Such was the irony of fate that there was a poster on the wall in that cabin with his picture and the caption, "Free Nazım Hikmet!"' says Janina Małachowska, a close friend of the poet.

For several hours Erduran and Hikmet wait for a decision. The captain calls Bucharest, and Bucharest calls Moscow, from where finally some instructions come through.

Hikmet goes to Romania, and from there to the USSR, where an enthusiastic welcome awaits him. Refik Erduran goes back to Istanbul in the little motorboat. For over twenty-five years he doesn't even tell his wife about his adventure.

stalin

1

In Moscow everyone panders to Hikmet. At the airport he is greeted by representatives of the regime and the most distinguished Soviet artistes.

But no one has the courage to take him to see Stalin.

The Turk is famous for his plain speaking, and Stalinist Moscow is extremely different from the place he remembers from his student days. The theatres only put on plays by Joseph

Vissarionovich's acolytes. The whole country is filled with statues of him.

Hikmet, who has spent a dozen years in prison, knows nothing about Stalinism. He is surprised Meyerhold and Mayakovsky are no longer alive. The former, an outstanding theatre director and innovator, was shot during the Stalinist purges. The latter, a phenomenal poet, died in unexplained circumstances, though according to the official version he committed suicide.

Hikmet is even more surprised to hear that many of his friends from his student days have died when only just in their fifties. Asked by his Soviet comrades which of the living ones he would like to see, he chooses innovative film director Nikolai Ekk.*

This causes the authorities considerable consternation. Ekk has been blacklisted and is not making films any more, on top of which he has become severely alcoholic and – according to the poet Yevgeny Yevtushenko – he stinks like an old dog.

However, his comrades get him into a suitable state to be shown to the guest from abroad, they file his nails, shove a bunch of flowers into his hand and take him to see Hikmet.

'What are you doing for the cinema, dear friend?' asks Nazım.

'For some reason lately I've been focusing more on the circus,' replies Ekk.

---

* Nikolai Vladimirovich Ekk (1902-1976) directed films including the first Soviet sound film, *Road to Life* (1931), which won an award at the 1932 Venice International Film Festival, and also the first films in colour. Stalin's death enabled him to return to work and to experiment with three-dimensional film. For more on Hikmet's life in Russia see: E. Timmes, S Göksu, *Romantic Communist, The Life and Work of Nazım Hikmet*, London, 2006.

2

Hikmet waits patiently for Stalin to find time for him. Two days before the appointed date he attends a reception given in his honour. He has been in the USSR long enough by now for it to have become evident that he cannot bear the local atmosphere. He can see through all the sycophancy and insincerity from miles away. He has devoted his entire life to the fight for communism, but this is not how he imagined it.

At the reception he listens patiently to the tributes paid to him by other men of letters, until finally it is his turn to speak. 'Brothers, I spent years in prison dreaming of the Moscow theatres... Moscow was a street revolution that changed into a stage revolution. But what do I see here nowadays? A play that's lacking in taste, called socialist realism. I see an incredible amount of toadying. How can toadying be revolutionary? In a few days' time I am to meet with Comrade Stalin. I intend to tell him frankly, as one communist to another, that these endless portraits and statues should be removed.'

On hearing these words, several people slip away from the reception in terror. To lighten the tone, the host says that Stalin probably dislikes some of his statues too, and quickly raises a toast to him.

3

A day later Hikmet receives a phone call from the Kremlin. Via his courtiers, Comrade Stalin informs him that he is terribly busy and must call off the meeting.

4

The poet never did have his meeting with Stalin, but that does not mean Stalin had forgotten about him.

The Generalissimus died in 1953. Two years later Hikmet invited Yevgeny Yevtushenko and another young poet to his *dacha* outside Moscow.

'He disconnected the phone and locked the door,' Yevtushenko tells the story. 'But history broke down that door and forced its way inside.' It took the form of a mildly tipsy elderly man, who fell on his knees before Hikmet.

'Nazım, forgive me!' he cried, and began to weep. 'There's something I have to confess!'

Nazım raised the man to his feet and said: 'You don't have to do anything.'

But the man felt he should.

When Hikmet first landed in Moscow, this man was assigned to him as a driver. The poet immediately reduced the distance between them, and they became friends. They would visit each other's homes, and have an occasional drink together.

Less than a year later the driver ended up in the Lubyanka, where he was interrogated by secret police chief Lavrentiy Beria in person.

'Do you know who you're driving?' asked Beria.

'A great poet… A friend of the Soviet Union,' replied the terrified driver, trying to guess the interrogator's intentions.

'He's no friend!' screamed Beria. 'He wants to kill Comrade Stalin. But we're going to kill him! Or to be precise, you are,' said Beria, pointing a finger at the driver.

Neither torture nor threats could persuade the driver. Only when his wife ended up at the Lubyanka did he agree to cooperate. From that moment on, day and night he had been waiting for the signal from Beria's people.

Four times he received a call to say he was to kill Hikmet, and four times the order was revoked.

'Nazım heard out this story with a stony expression,' says Yevtushenko. 'Finally he said: "There's really nothing to talk about. Better pour the vodka."'

gota

Hikmet can tell that as long as Stalin is resident in the Kremlin, he'd better stay as far away from Moscow as possible. He becomes a great promoter of the Committee for the Defence of Peace, travelling the world, gracing congresses with his presence and cutting ribbons. He makes his first appearance in Warsaw only a few months after escaping from Turkey.

The Polish defenders of peace select a Turkologist called Małgorzata Łabęcka-Koecherowa to be his interpreter. Known for short as Gota, she wrote her master's dissertation on Hikmet. Now ninety-three, Gota recalls how when she started working with the poet she had to establish the rules of the game clearly right away.

'He was terribly fond of women, so I told him: "You are my *abi*." In Turkish that means an older brother, who is responsible for the entire family. He liked that very much, and our relationship became clear cut,' she tells me, and adds: 'He was like a child. Pure goodness, and at the same time naïve. If you met him in the street and asked him for some money, he'd give you the lot.'

Yevtushenko has a similar memory of Hikmet. Once the Turk called him to ask if he needed any money.

'I didn't,' says Yevtushenko. 'And I hurt Nazım's feelings by saying so. "Are you sure?" he asked. "That's a pity... I got a money order today and it's definitely too much for me."'

According to Gota: 'He earned a lot, but he was happy if he managed to get rid of the money as soon as possible. He would give it away to anyone who asked him. He was the kindest man I've ever known.'

borzęcki

1

Stalin is in no hurry to give the poet Soviet citizenship. Meanwhile, he has lost his Turkish citizenship by fleeing the country. This is a serious impediment, because Hikmet wants to travel the world. His Warsaw friends know about his Polish great-grandfather, so with Gota's help, they try to get him a Polish passport on that basis.

Polish communist leader Bolesław Bierut, who enjoys the occasional chat with Hikmet, has nothing against this plan. Does he consult the Kremlin about it? It is hard to say, but he probably does. The fact is that in 1952 General Celaleddin's great-grandson is granted Polish citizenship and a passport in the name of Nazım Hikmet Borzęcki.

Who signed the authorisation? It must have been the Council of State, and Bierut himself probably appended his signature, but in the state archives there is no trace of this document.

However, a People's Republic of Poland passport with a photo of the poet, smiling faintly, is kept at the Hikmet Museum in Istanbul. The poet has tried to sign his name as Borzęcki, but judging from the crooked letters, he evidently wasn't used to that name.

The document becomes extremely useful in 1956, when the so-called thaw prevails in Poland, and Władysław Gomułka comes to power. The Poles believe that the Polish version of socialism is finally starting to be built, and their enthusiasm infects Hikmet too. He is delighted by Gomułka, and spends more than a year in Warsaw. His biographers write in unison that these were the beginnings of the sort of communism he had in mind.

According to Polish poet Andrzej Mandalian: 'He spoke highly of the atmosphere in Poland. The USSR at that time was rife with awful graphomania, but we valued artistic freedom. He liked that very much.'

Did he feel himself to be in the least bit Polish? In 1958, at a meeting with readers at the International Press and Book Club he says: 'I have a Polish nose, hair that was blond before it went grey, and a large dose of what may be Polish Romanticism.'

A year later in an interview for the weekly *Orka* he adds: 'With various countries to choose from, I chose the land of my grandfather.'

But he tells his friends it was an inevitable choice.

2

During the thaw Hikmet becomes a member of the Polish Writers' Union. The lady archivist has a problem with him – he did not fill in his own form providing personal details. Also his file of documents, articles and correspondence is extremely thin. Others, even the mediocre poets, have fat files. The eminent poets have several files each, and they're bulky.

Hikmet's file consists of two letters from fans, the decision to accept him as a member of the Union ('Astonishing,' the lady archivist tells me, 'because members ought to be living and writing in Poland') and one photograph. In it, Hikmet is wearing a shirt with a folk pattern and is chatting to the writer Wiktor Woroszylski. Behind them Marcel Reich-Ranicki is smoking a cigarette, a Jew who survived the ghetto and was a future luminary of German literary criticism.

3

Hikmet's file is not the only slender thing about him. Human memory is equally thin.

According to Polish poet Julia Hartwig: 'He was tall, well-built, and very nice. He used to dine at the Writers' Union canteen. I can't help you more than that because that's all I can remember.'

'[Poet Julian] Tuwim was delighted by him,' says Andrzej Mandalian. 'He was very sensitive to the sound of speech, and Hikmet could recite beautifully in Turkish. Unfortunately, I don't remember anything else about him either.'

Gota mentions that Nazım befriended Władysław Broniewski, a poet from Płock, who in those days was a heavy drinker. Hikmet's friends were afraid he would encourage the Turk – with his weak heart – to drink.

Unfortunately, apart from some poems translated from Russian, I cannot find any evidence of this friendship anywhere.

It is a similar story with the diaries and notes of other Polish writers. Neither Adam Ważyk, nor Antoni Słonimski nor Jarosław Iwaszkiewicz mentions him. Poet and short story writer Iwaszkiewicz knew Hikmet well. He translated several of his poems into Polish and was active among the defenders of peace. I call his daughter Maria:

'What's the name? Hikmet? No, it doesn't ring a bell.'

Our writers have a distinct problem with Hikmet, if not two problems. The first? They are already feeling detached from communism, whereas he isn't in the least. He spent the war and the greater part of Stalinism in a Turkish prison, daydreaming about communist Moscow. There are lots of things he doesn't know, and there are lots he doesn't want to know. Even though he has seen for himself what Stalin got up to, he has not taken the smallest step away from communism.

The second problem is to do with his poetry. According to the propaganda, he is one of the greatest poets in the world. He is their colleague at the Union, and he dines with them there, but they don't find his poetry all that great.

Another Polish poet, Julian Przyboś, comments that Hikmet's poetry 'is too archaic to gain a following in Poland'. Whereas in a review of one of his collections Julia Hartwig writes that Hikmet is badly translated. She insists that he should be translated from Turkish in a continuous stream, like prose.

Gota, who at this time already has a monopoly on translating Hikmet, scathingly reminds her that when she translated the poems of Chairman Mao she did not turn them into prose.

Yet to domesticate their new colleague the Polish writers compare him to their greatest national bard, Adam Mickiewicz. Firstly, because Mickiewicz died in Istanbul, and secondly because just as Mickiewicz was homesick for Poland, Hikmet too pined for Turkey in a beautiful way:

> My country, my country!
> No longer do I have a Turkish worker's cap,
> No longer do I have the shoes I wore in my homeland;
> long ago I tore the last shirt
> made of cloth woven in Şile.

The comparison sounds interesting. But the Turk himself shatters it – when the journalists ask for his opinion of Mickiewicz, he says he hasn't got one. He has never read any of his works.

gala

Since his youth Hikmet has been ill with serious heart disease. In 1953 he suffers a severe heart attack, and the doctors only just manage to save him.

But like a real Turkish macho man he does not waste any time convalescing. At the sanatorium he takes a youthful lady doctor by the arm, and they go for a cup of coffee. From now on they will have coffee together every day. Doctor Galina Kolesnikova becomes Hikmet's partner, doctor and girlfriend, and travels to Poland, Czechoslovakia, East Germany and Hungary with him.

In Warsaw they stay at the Sejm (the parliament building).

According to Janina Małachowska, a close friend of Hikmet's: 'I worked in the office there. Hikmet complained that he and Gala had very little space at their hotel. His name opened lots of doors, so I sorted out a guest room for them. We used to meet almost every day at the Sejm restaurant. The waitress, whose name was Marysia, used to say: "Hikmet or not, what a fine figure of a man!"'

Gala gazes at him in worship like an icon. Hikmet treats this homage as something perfectly natural, which annoys Gota, who encourages Gala to stir up a bit of jealousy in the poet.

'Don't keep trailing after him. Go and have a coffee with some other man, and then tell him how nice it was,' she says. Gala listens as if bewitched.

A few weeks later, accompanied by Gota and Małachowska, she takes Hikmet to another sanatorium. He takes Galina by the hand, and she pours out her story: 'Nazım, Gota says I'm to go and have coffee with someone else. But I don't want to, because I love you so much I could even kiss your arse!'

münevver

Nowadays Hikmet would have been the darling of the gutter press.

Three of his four wives left their former husbands for him. Not even the most powerful calculator on earth could add up the total number of his affairs.

Yet the greatest publicity came from Hikmet's marriage to Münevver Andaç, his uncle's daughter.

Turkologist Tadeusz Majda was a friend of hers. 'She was a very beautiful, elegant woman,' he says. 'She had an incredible intellect and a lovely low voice, typical of women from the Turkish aristocracy.'

Münevver visits Nazım while he is still in prison. When he is released, she runs away from her first husband, taking her daughter Renan with her. Soon after, Münevver falls pregnant again – by Hikmet, and they get married.

Nazım's escape from the country is like the October Revolution in her life. The Turkish authorities are furious, and the only way they can annoy Hikmet is by harassing his loved ones. Münevver is summoned to endless interrogations, her house is under surveillance, her friends are afraid to meet up with her, and nobody wants to give her a job.

For the first few years Nazım writes Münevver very loving, homesick letters. His most beautiful poems are all about how much he misses her and their little son. Galina knows that her happiness by the poet's side will only last as long as Münevver is off the scene.

Later on, however, Hikmet's communications with his family start to wane. Finally they come to a virtual halt.

vera

1

The story of Hikmet's last great love is as follows.

His friend Ekber Babayev introduces him to two women who work for Mosfilm. They want to consult him about some Albanian folk costumes, and to take the opportunity to meet the eminent Turk.

'The blonde isn't bad, but she's flat-chested,' Hikmet tells Babayev. They are talking in Tatar. Neither of the ladies can possibly understand what they're talking about.

Except that the blonde with the flat chest was hidden in a Tatar village during the war, and knows the language well enough to cause Hikmet major embarrassment.

Her name is Vera Tulyakova.

2

Hikmet turns up at Vera's place for the first time to help correct the screenplay. And then for the second time – with a bunch of flowers – to take her out for a cup of coffee.

Vera has a husband. That has never been an obstacle to Hikmet. Stalin's daughter, Svetlana Alliluyeva, even called him a romantic communist.

But it is an obstacle to Vera.

Hikmet pursues her for several years. He tempts her with offers to collaborate on screenplays and to go on trips abroad with him, and he keeps sending her flowers. After suffering from writer's block for some years he starts writing poetry again.

Vera finally breaks down while Hikmet is away in Warsaw. She calls to say she wants to see him. He packs his bags, cancels all his meetings and that very evening boards the train back to Moscow.

A few days later he runs away from Galina through a window, in nothing but his socks.

'He hadn't the courage to tell me the truth,' Galina explains to me over the phone. 'For months I wept all day and all night long.'

Nazım and Vera go to Paris. Meanwhile the furious Galina sweeps through Hikmet's flat like a tornado. She leaves a huge mess and a card saying: 'To hell with both of you.'

3

Hikmet's friends did not like Vera.

'There was something about her that we found off-putting,' says Janina Małachowska. 'Galina was all right, very friendly. She even used to buy clothes for Münevver and her children, because she knew they weren't exactly rolling in it over there, whereas Vera was very haughty.'

Others recall how he and Vera destroyed the carefully constructed myth that Nazım was like a suffering Odysseus, kept apart from his Penelope by an evil fate.

Especially when his Penelope miraculously turned up at the Hotel Bristol in Warsaw. It happened like this:

joyce

In early 1961 Hikmet goes to Stockholm to honour a conference of the Committee for the Defence of Peace with his presence. There Italian writer and translator Joyce Salvadori Lussu catches his eye, a legend in the anti-fascist resistance movement.

They have a cup of coffee and a chat together. Hikmet reads her his poems and urges her to translate them into Italian.

But what makes the biggest impression on Lussu is the story of his wife.

She decides to take action. She flies to Istanbul and visits Münevver. She notices that the walls of her modest flat are plastered from top to bottom in pictures of Nazım. She and Münevver work out an escape plan. Joyce asks her friend, the millionaire Carlo Giullini, for help.

'For once in your life do something for others!' she tells him. Giullini laughs and agrees. He sails his yacht to Turkey, and Joyce escorts Münevver and her children to the harbour in the small town of Ayvalık.

That night they sail away towards the Greek island of Lesbos. Halfway there, they run into a storm. The wind tears the sails and tosses the boat about. A wave inundates the deck and everyone falls into the water. Death is only a whisker away.

They are rescued by some Greek fishermen. Münevver reports to the immigration office, where she claims to be Polish, with the surname Borzęcki. She says her documents have been lost at sea. Thanks to the defenders of peace, the Polish authorities confirm her story.

A few days later Münevver sends Joyce a telegram from Warsaw: 'Everything's fine.'

That is only partly true.

münevver

1

Nazım is not at the airport to meet his family. Münevver is greeted at Warsaw airport by Gota, who takes her to the Hotel Bristol on Krakowskie Przedmieście in the city centre.

The poet turns up the next day, at breakfast. He flies in straight from Havana, where he went to present Fidel Castro with an award – naturally – from the defenders of peace.

For the first time Münevver finds out that her husband is with another woman.

2

After this Nazım and Münevver only ever talk about poetry.

3

Hikmet wants Münevver to settle in Leipzig in East Germany, where he can get her a job at the Turkish radio station.

But Münevver would rather stay in Warsaw. She and the children adopt the surname Borzęcki, and the defenders of peace fix her up with a flat in the Old Town.

Tadeusz Majda, then a junior lecturer and now a professor at Warsaw University's Faculty of Oriental Studies, is surprised to discover that for the first time in its history the faculty is going to have a lector from Turkey. Then to his even greater surprise he learns that the lector is the wife of the famous Nazım Hikmet.

For eight years Münevver lectures at Warsaw University. She and Majda produce a course book for learning Turkish, and with Gota and Stanisława Płaskowicka-Rymiewicz she publishes a *History of Turkish Literature*.

To this day this book is required reading for all young Turkologists.

4

Joyce Salvadori Lussu's excellent intentions were not appreciated.

Still in Warsaw, Nazım writes her a letter saying she deserves to go to heaven, even if 'the Pope wouldn't agree'. Then he cites the tale of the Kurdish shepherd who ends up at a rich man's abode. The rich man hosts him generously, and the Kurd knows he'll never be able to pay him back. This bothers him so much that he decides to cut his benefactor's throat.

'I feel like that Kurd,' Hikmet ends his letter.

Münevver's letter to Joyce is even more bitter: 'Now Nazım is like a pasha with two wives. And I am the foolish one...'

Years later Joyce recalled: 'The story of his beloved wife and their son, which broke all our hearts, had sunk like a stone to the bottom of a well.'

pamuk

Münevver leaves Poland during the anti-Semitic campaign of 1968. No one drives her out, though she has inherited a large dose of Jewish blood from her mother, but she is disgusted by the atmosphere that has come to prevail in Poland.

In Paris she translates Turkish literature, including almost all of Hikmet, into French. Her translations are regarded as brilliant. The fact that Hikmet gained a large amount of fame in Paris is mainly thanks to his ex-wife.

In the early 1980s she is the first to appreciate the talents of the young Orhan Pamuk. She translates his work, and opens the door to the West for him.

'You don't have to know French to sense how brilliant these translations are,' says the Nobel prize-winning writer Pamuk of Münevver.

memed

1

> My country – on the opposite shore
> I call to you I call from Varna
> Memed Memed
> Can you hear my voice Memed
> The Black Sea keeps on flowing
> O furious yearning, mad longing
> O son, I cry, can you hear me calling you from Varna
> Memed Memed

writes Hikmet while on a trip to Bulgaria.

He only has one child, his son by Münevver, whose name is Memed Hikmet. When the poet fled his homeland, Memed was just a babe in arms.

Above the bed in Hikmet's house in Moscow hang two large photos of the smiling Memed in a striped shirt. The poet sometimes spends hours on end lying on the bed, gazing at his son.

2

Memed Hikmet talks about their meeting at the Hotel Bristol in Warsaw in an interview published by the Turkish newspaper *Milliyet* in the 1970s. It is the only interview he ever gave.

During their first meeting Nazım recites poetry and tells a few anecdotes from Cuba. He doesn't ask Memed any questions; in fact he hardly takes any notice of him. For the boy, who has been brought up to worship his father, it must be a shock.

Later on Memed gets the impression that his father is flirting with a woman sitting a few tables away, and 'seems satisfied to find that despite his advanced age he is still attractive' (at the time Hikmet was just over fifty).

3

While Hikmet is talking to Münnever, Memed and Renan are taken care of by Gota's daughters, Barbara and Agnieszka.

'We used to take him for walks, sometimes to Łazienki Park, sometimes to the Old Town,' says Agnieszka Koecher-Hensel. She remembers that he couldn't pronounce various Polish words properly.

Münnever has a lot of work in Poland, so Memed ends up at a boarding school for diplomats' children. He learns Polish at lightning speed, both the more and the less literary kind, but is not always capable of telling the difference between them.

'After he'd spent a year at the boarding school we went on holiday to stay with my aunt in Krynica Morska,' says Koecher-Hensel. 'Memed enthusiastically described how he'd taken part in a spiritualist séance, during which they managed to summon up a ghost, to which my aunt said: "Memed, there's no such things as ghosts!" And Memed replied: "I wonder what you'd say if your teacup started talking bullshit, Auntie?"'

vera

1

When Hikmet falls in love with Vera, a doctor friend warns him: 'If you let yourself go ahead with this affair, you won't last for more than three years.' Hikmet just smiles.

In 1960 he gets his long awaited Soviet passport, so finally he can tie the knot with Verochka. As they set off for the registry office, the driver asks: 'Comrade Hikmet, if you spent all those years in jail, how come you want to get stuck in another form of slavery?' Again, Hikmet just smiles.

2

Nazım Hikmet Borzęcki died on 3rd June 1963 – exactly three years and two months after his wedding to Vera. Twelve years had gone by since his escape from Turkey. To the day he died, he never set foot on Turkish soil again.

memed

1

> Memed,
> my son,
> I leave you in the care
> of the Turkish Communist Party.
> I go
> at peace.
> The life that's coming to an end in me
> will survive for a time in you*

Nazım leaves not just his son to the Turkish Communist Party, but also a quarter share of the copyrights to his works. Münnever and Memed get the other three-quarters, and Vera's share of the inheritance is the *dacha* outside Moscow.

At the funeral Memed bravely endures hours and hours of speeches. Only when he is told to kiss his father just before the coffin is closed, does he burst into a fit of sobbing.

For the next five years he and his mother regularly take part in events commemorating his father, sometimes at the International Press and Book Club, sometimes at the Writers' House.

In 1968 they leave for Paris together. Memed becomes a

---

* *Poems of Nazım Hikmet*, op. cit.

painter. In the early 1980s Barbara Łabęcka, Gota's older sister, pays them a visit.

'Münnever lived modestly. I'm not much of a talker, and she wasn't very effusive either, so we were having rather a hard time making conversation. As soon as Memed arrived, I breathed a sigh of relief. We took the metro together afterwards and he kept asking: "Is my Polish still all right? I haven't lost my Mokotów accent, have I?" I had no idea what a Mokotów accent was, but I didn't want to hurt his feelings, so I said he hadn't.'

2

In 1996 Münnever Borzęcka dies.

In 2002 Memed Hikmet Borzęcki applies to have his Turkish citizenship restored, and his application is approved. These days he divides his time between Istanbul and Paris. He is at odds with a large number of his relatives, who cannot understand why he refuses to talk about his great father.

I was eager to meet Memed. I managed to locate some Turkish and Parisian friends of his, and two of his schoolmates from Poland, who claim to be still in touch with him. I also tracked down Renan, his half-sister, who spent the first few years in Poland with him, and who now lives in Istanbul.

But all in vain – Memed's friends refused to hear of putting me in touch with him, and they kept dotting their memories of him with the remark: 'That's not for print, that's not for print either'. But a few days later – perhaps after communicating with Memed – they forbade me to quote our conversations at all.

Initially, Renan invited me to dinner, but just before it she apologised and withdrew the invitation.

Every time I came a step closer to Memed, I bumped up against the impenetrable wall he has built to separate himself from journalists, as if the very thought of having to talk about his father caused him great pain. As if in his early years there were too many of those pompous celebrations, processions, meetings at the International Press and Book Club and admirers in love with his great father. As if he wanted to cut himself off entirely from the fact that he is the son of Nazım Hikmet, the great poet and communist: the man who wasn't afraid of prison or of Stalin; who handed out money left and right; but who was a total failure as a husband and as a father.

vera

A week after Hikmet's death a poem is found in his jacket, 'To Vera':

Come she said
Stay she said
Smile she said
Die she said
I came
I stayed
I smiled
I died*

Ten years later, the Turkish government takes him off the blacklist, and his poems can be published in Istanbul. Hikmetomania begins – a major fashion for his poetry, which continues to this day.

In 2008, on the centenary of his birth, an acclaimed Turkish composer writes an oratorio in his honour. Almost every book with his name in the title sells thousands of copies, and the same goes for CDs of music written to accompany his poems. He has several dozen fan club pages on Facebook, and a small Hikmet museum has been established in Istanbul. More than

---

* *Ibid.*

ten independent committees are fighting for permission to erect a statue of him.

Early in 2009, forty-six years after Hikmet's death, the Turkish government rehabilitates him and restores his citizenship. Another dozen committees fight to bring his remains back to Turkey. Their rationale is that Hikmet was homesick for his country, and in one of his poems he wrote that he wanted to be buried there.

But their efforts are doomed to failure because the decision has to have the support of his closest relatives. Meanwhile, through his lawyer, the poet's only son has said that his father should remain buried in Moscow.

that's turkey for you

LATELY bathing suits for Muslim women have been a huge hit in Turkey. They completely cover the legs and arms, and have sweet little hoods to go over the head. Most of them also have a matching cape, so the material won't hug the body and reveal the ins and outs of the figure.

'It's not perfect,' Emina, a mother of three, tells the newspaper *Milliyet*. 'My one gets filled with water and forms a sort of large balloon. But at last I can swim! Not so long ago I could only watch my family playing in the water, like a cat gazing at frying liver.'

'Ever since I got married, I haven't been able to go to the swimming pool or the beach,' complains Fatma, a housewife from the east of Turkey. 'Now I've got to remember how to swim all over again. But I'm very pleased. It's a small thing, but it makes me happy.'

The bathing trunks for men have longer than standard legs. According to Mehmet Şahin, owner of a company called Haşema and designer of the first costumes: 'When I was a student I felt very embarrassed going to the beach. In classic bathing trunks I felt as if I were naked. That was when it occurred to me – this is a gap in the market! A few years later I began production of the first costumes.'

The Muslim female swimmers have stirred a good deal of

commotion at Turkish resorts, leading to a number of fights between modern, pro-Western Turks and the religious ones who have spoiled the first lot's view as well as their fun.

So the newspaper *Hürriyet* published a picture of two women standing side by side, up to their waists in water. One was in a Muslim costume, covering everything except her eyes. The other was topless.

'That's Turkey for you,' ran the editorial commentary.

about the author

WITOLD SZABŁOWSKI is an award-winning Polish journalist and writer. After a period studying and working in Istanbul he came to specialise in Turkish affairs, but also writes about Central Europe and the Balkan countries. In 2008, he won a prestigious Polish journalism prize, the Melchior Wańkowicz Award, in the 'Inspiration of the Year'; category. His report on Turkish honour killings, *It's Out of Love, Sister*, received an honorary mention at the Amnesty International competition for the best articles on human rights issues. In 2010, he received the European Parliament Journalism Award for his reportage *The Purgatory of Istanbul*. Both reports are included in this book. In the 2012 edition of the Anna Lindh Mediterranean Journalist Award he won a Special Mention for his report on Albanian migration, *Let Us In, You Bastards!* (to be found at http://nextinline.eu/let-us-in-you-bastards/).

about the translator

ANTONIA LLOYD-JONES is a full-time translator of Polish literature. Her published translations include fiction by several of Poland's leading contemporary novelists, including *The Last Supper* by Paweł Huelle, for which she won the Found in Translation Award 2008. Her translations of non-fiction include reportage, literary biographies and essays. She also translates poetry and books for children. In 2012 she won the Found in Translation Award again for her body of work that year.